LOVE'S MIND

ALSO BY JOHN S. DUNNE

The City of the Gods

A Search for God in Time and Memory

The Way of All the Earth

Time and Myth

The Reasons of the Heart

The Church of the Poor Devil

The House of Wisdom

The Homing Spirit

The Peace of the Present

LOVE'S MIND

An Essay on Contemplative Life

JOHN S. DUNNE

UNIVERSITY OF NOTRE DAME PRESS

Notre Dame   London

Library of Congress Cataloging-in-Publication Data

Dunne, John S., 1929–
    Love's mind : an essay on contemplative life / John S. Dunne.
      p. cm.
    Includes bibliographical references and index.
    ISBN 0-268-01303-9 (alk. paper)
    1. Contemplation.   2. Christianity and the arts.   3. Spiritual
life—Catholic Church.   4. Catholic Church—Doctrines.
I. Title.
BV5091.C7D86   1993
248.3'4—dc20   93-13910
                                              CIP

Contents

Preface   vii

A Late Summer Night's Dream   1

The Friends of God   9
    A Guiding Presence   10
    A Guarding Presence   20

The Words and the Music   31
    The Way of Words   32
    The Way of Music   42

Three Movements of Contemplation   53
    The Restless Heart   54
    Heart Speaks to Heart   63
    Following the Heart   72

The Lovers of God   83
    Remembering Love   84
    Love's Road   94

Love's Mind   107

Two Song Cycles   123
    Ayasofya   125
    Songs about Songs   134

Notes   141

Index   155

Preface

Ours is a violent city, I believe, because one of the three lives of the ancient city, action and contemplation and enjoyment, is missing, the life of contemplation, and its empty place is taken and filled by violence. I name contemplation *Love's Mind* here, taking the phrase from *A Midsummer Night's Dream*, though Shakespeare doesn't think love has much of a mind. There is something of the mind, nevertheless, in matters of the heart, something that comes to mind as the heart's longing becomes knowing, as unknowing love becomes knowing. It is this mind in matters of the heart that is the substance of contemplative life.

I began writing over a summer with a chapter called "The Friends of God." I was thinking of a conversation I had long ago with a friend who told me, "You see life as a journey with God, but I see it as a wrestling with God." It is true, I see life as a journey with God in time, but getting into situations I would not have chosen I begin to see it as a wrestling with God. A friend of God sees life as a journey with God, I think, but a lover of God is likely to see it as a wrestling with God. So it is that I saw my book as the story of a friend of God becoming a lover of God, and I planned to go from an opening chapter on the friends to a closing chapter on the lovers. At the end of the summer, however, I had a dream in which I asked the question, "Do we love with a love we know or with a love we do not know?" And the answer came, "with a love we do not know." Then I saw I had the real beginning of my book. "A Late Summer Night's Dream" I called it and went on to compare it with Shakespeare's dream of a midsummer night. I saw the book then as a story of unknowing love that becomes knowing when it comes to the realization Shakespeare speaks of, "Mine own, and not mine own." Unknowing love becomes knowing as it becomes heart-free.

I saw myself and all of us as unknowing lovers of God, led on by our heart's longing from one thing to another, from one person to another. Here I found a connection with Mozart, somewhat like that with Shakespeare. There is a kind of worldliness about Mozart and Shakespeare that has always intrigued me. "Bach and Beethoven walked with God," it has been said. "Mozart did not. Mozart danced with the masked daughters of Vienna." Yet there are depths in Mozart, even if they are "black depths" of melancholy. I see or, listening, I hear the unrequited longing of the heart in this melancholy, the longing that becomes the love of God. There is a way of words and a way of music, I have come to believe, and so I wrote the chapter "The Words and the Music." I had chosen the way of words many years ago, but now for me it has rejoined the way of music, and I have taken to composing again, as I did when I was a teenager and have even included here the lyrics of two song cycles I have written, "Ayasofya" and "Songs about Songs."

Music for me is new life, music combining with words, and spiritual friendship is new life, friendship combining with new awareness of the love of God. There are "Three Movements of Contemplation," I go on to say in the book. There is the restless movement of the heart from one thing to another when it becomes a conscious process of saying "not this, not that" (the *neti neti* of the Upanishads), and there is the movement of heart speaking to heart (Newman's *cor ad cor loquitur*), and there is the movement of following the heart (Marcel's subordination of self to "a reality at my deepest level more truly me than I am myself"). As I see them, these are three phases in passing from longing to love, from the restless longing of the heart, I mean, to the love of God. I see these movements, or hear them, in the many song cycles I mention throughout, from Schubert's

Winter Journey to Tolkien's *The Road Goes Ever On.* It is as if the movements of contemplation were three movements of a musical composition. And I see them as the essential movements of a friendship as it becomes spiritual.

When I came then to write of "The Lovers of God," I wrote of "Remembering Love," with the thought that love of God is already there in us as heart's longing, but when I wrote of "Love's Road" I found myself translating the poetry of Saint John of the Cross from Spanish to English, trying by translating to enter into it in a way I never had before. It is Saint John of the Cross who speaks of the road of the heart's desire as "the road of the union of love with God." I know this is my road, and it is the road of spiritual friendship where the love of God becomes something conscious among human friends. I found the poetry of Saint John spoke to my heart in a way that his prose did not, but I consulted his prose to discover what I had missed in his poetry. He is purely and simply in love with God; I am rather on the way from longing to love. Something close to his "night of sense" and "night of spirit" that spoke directly to my condition I found in John Donne's poem "Negative Love" set to music by John Adams. For "negative love" that says "not this, not that" is longing that is becoming love.

"Love's Mind," I conclude, if I may include the heart's longing as well as the love of God, is contemplation that runs the gamut of human experience, from restlessness to rest in God. It is Aristotle who speaks of three lives, enjoyment and action and contemplation, in his *Nicomachean Ethics* and sees happiness above all in the life of contemplation, the life of the intellectual virtues. I am getting my conception of the contemplative life more from Aquinas, where it has a more religious cast but the substance of it comes from Augustine and his thought "our heart is restless until it rests in you." In fact, by including the restlessness of the heart I want to see contemplation as bridge between action and enjoyment and to see a legitimacy also in enjoyment. I am influenced here by George Steiner's *Real Presences*, (University of Chicago Press, 1989), his argument that art and literature and music point to God. I feel myself being led to a vision like Augustine's of the city of God, the vision of a city of the heart where contemplation again takes the place of violence.

Although I am writing here about contemplative life as a dimension of every human life, not about monastic life, I have learned a lot about the life of contemplation from giving retreats over the last twelve years in Trappist monasteries, at Gethsemane and Lafayette and Conyers and Spencer, also at the Camaldolese monastery at Big Sur and at the Carmel in Elysburgh. My thanks go to the Trappists, the Camaldolese, the Carmelites, for inviting me and for showing me the way. Also I have learned from our Wellfleet meetings on Cape Cod, and especially from the time when I was invited to give a presentation on violence and the contemplative life, and again just lately on contemplative life as the missing dimension in American life. My thanks go especially to Robert Jay Lifton and Betty Jean Lifton, who hosted those meetings. As in *Love's Labour's Lost* we learn to be "still and contemplative in living art."

A Late Summer Night's Dream

Once in a dream on a late summer night I met Saint Thomas Aquinas and asked him a question. He was in a high place in the mountains, looking out over the prospect. He was dressed like a modern mountain climber, not in his friar's habit, and he looked nothing like the paintings we have of him. Yet I knew it was he. I knelt beside him, looking out myself over the prospect. "Tell me about love," I said. "Do we love with a love we know or with a love we do not know?"

"With a love we do not know," I believe he answered, though my memory of the dream is not sure at this point. When I awakened and thought about the dream, I thought his answer in life, according to his writings, would have been more careful. "We participate in God's love," he might have said, "and so we know and we don't know. We know in that we really do partake of the divine love. We don't know in that divine love is something greater than ourselves."[1]

If I had asked Shakespeare that question, he too might have replied "with a love we do not know," but his meaning is different:

> Things base and vile, holding no quantity,
> Love can transpose to form and dignity.
> Love looks not with the eyes, but with the mind,
> And therefore is wing'd Cupid painted blind.
> Nor hath Love's mind of any judgement taste;
> Wings and no eyes figure unheedy haste:

1

And therefore Love is said to be a child,
Because in choice he is so oft beguil'd.[2]

Helena, in love with Demetrius, has these lines in *A Midsummer Night's Dream.* There is a quadrangle of love in the play, Helena in love with Demetrius, and he with Hermia, and she with Lysander, and he with her. All it takes is an enchantment worked by Puck to turn Lysander's love to Helena, and then the quadrangle becomes a circle, and every man is in love with a woman who does not love him, and every woman is in love with a man who does not love her, and all love is unrequited. The image of "love's mind" is Titania, queen of the fairies, in love by enchantment with Bottom whose head has become that of an ass. Titania and Bottom are like a parody of Beauty and the Beast. Her love indeed "can transpose" the man with the head of an ass "to form and dignity"; she "looks not with the eyes, but with the mind"; nor does her mind in its "unheedy haste" have "of any judgement taste," for "in choice" she is "beguil'd." All is set to rights, nevertheless, when Demetrius is enchanted and falls in love with Helena, and when Lysander and Titania are disenchanted and come to their senses, and so in the end, the happy ending of comedy, all lovers are happy.

A thought occurs to me as I set my own dream beside Shakespeare's dream. It is that our being in love may be God loving in us, and that our blind love may be God's unconditional love in us. Love at its most unknowing may be in accord with love at its most knowing. I don't mean knowing makes no difference. Knowing, according to Aquinas, brings the things we know into us, but loving takes us out to the things we love. Knowing and loving are our two basic relationships with things, knowing is taking things in and loving is going out to things. But loving without knowing mistakes the identity of the one loved, mistakes the man with the ass head for someone who is wise and beautiful. A loving that is knowing, on the other hand, may find wisdom and beauty where it seems lacking, as Beauty does in the Beast.

What is required for a loving that is knowing, for a knowing that is loving, is "the quiet eye."

A quiet eye, "a way of looking at pictures,"[3] as Sylvia Judson describes it, is also, as she says, a way of looking on life. It is an eye at rest, the opposite of a roving eye. It is the eye of contemplation, the eye of one who lives in peace. It is like the eye of a spectator at a play. Imagine the whole play of Shakespeare's dream done by only two actors, a man and a woman. They would play the royal pair, Theseus and Hippolyta, and the fairy pair, Oberon and Titania, and the comic pair, Pyramis and Thisbe, as well as the two pairs of young lovers, Lysander and Hermia, Demetrius and Helena. They couldn't do every scene. The dialogues of the two women, Hermia and Helena, and of the two men, Lysander and Demetrius, would become soliloquies, and scenes of more than two would be reduced to scenes of two. But the essentials would be there, for instance the scenes of Titania in love with Bottom with his head of an ass. And what is left, if it were clear to the audience that only two actors were involved, would appear to be a man and a woman in a series of guises and situations, just as happens in an actual human relationship. The eye of the spectator would be like the quiet eye that sees the unity of the person behind all the faces of circumstance.

Now imagine being not just a spectator but one of the participants in the story of love. "All the world's a stage, and all the men and women merely players,"[4] Shakespeare said. In an exchange of verses Ben Jonson asked,

> If, but stage actors, all the world displays,
> Where shall we find spectators of their plays?

and Shakespeare replied,

> Little, or much, of what we see, we do;
> We're all both actors and spectators too.

Let us imagine then being both players and spectators in the story of love. "The quiet eye" is the eye not just of a spectator but of a spectator who is also a player. It is the eye not just of a knower but of a knower who is also a lover.

This brings me back to my own dream in the mountains, looking out over the prospect and asking about love. Aquinas in the dream is not just a viewer of the mountains but a mountain climber, not just a spectator but a player. And so am I, I suppose, kneeling beside him and looking out over the prospect. There is a climb to reach the vantage point of his vision. And what is his vision? I think of a place in the Rocky Mountains where there is a grand vista and someone has carved on a rock the words "Be still, and know that I am God."[5] As it is formulated in his little essay *On Being and Essence*, Aquinas' vision begins with being and ends with God. It begins with the mountains, as it were, and ends with the stillness in which you know God is God. As it is formulated in his two *Summas*, it is a vision of everything coming from God and returning to God. I think of the old man Lawrence of Arabia met in the desert and his saying, "The love is from God, and of God, and towards God."[6] The vision of everything coming from God and going to God, as I understand it, is a vision of love. Thus in the dream, kneeling beside Aquinas and looking out with him over the mountains, surveying as it were the prospect of being, I said "Tell me about love."

If loving means going out to things, and knowing means taking things in, then there is "a circle in the acts of the soul,"[7] as Aquinas says, there is a knowing that comes of loving and there is a loving that comes of knowing. It is like the great circle of love coming from God and returning to God. In fact, as loving becomes knowing and knowing becomes loving, the circle of the soul becomes in us the great circle of the love of God. It is true, the peaceful feeling that comes with gazing at mountains seems very different from the troubled feeling that comes with love, and especially with unrequited love. If there is a circle here nonetheless in the acts of the soul, then perhaps the troubles of love can lead into the peace of wisdom and the roving eye can become the quiet eye. Here is the climb to the vantage point of vision. Love has to become free and untroubled.

Now therefore imagine Shakespeare's dream enacted by only one player, say by Helena who has the lines about "Love's mind." All the dialogues now become soliloquies. They become "a lover's discourse."[8] Helena is Helena whose love is unrequited and yet also Hermia whose love is requited and also Hippolyta whose love is captured and also Titania whose love is beguiled and also Thisbe whose love is tragicomic. Helena is already well on the way to wisdom in her discourse on "Love's mind." And when Demetrius is hers in the end by enchantment, she remarks

> And I have found Demetrius like a jewel,
> Mine own, and not mine own.[9]

Here is the high point of wisdom in the lover's discourse, "Mine own, and not mine own," the uncertainty principle of love. There is a having and a not having in love, as in treasure trove, as in something you find unexpectedly and you are not really certain it is yours. If I can live in that uncertainty without despairing, if I can say "Mine own, and not mine own" of all I love the most and know it is enough for me, then I can live in peace.

"Mine own, and not mine own." As I say those words myself, I feel the enormity of the letting be and of the openness to mystery, letting my own be not my own and being open to the mystery showing through the crack between "mine own" and "not mine own." There is something tantalizing here. Mystery, as Heidegger says, is "that which shows itself and at the same time withdraws."[10] That is what tantalizes me. There is something here that shows itself and at the same time withdraws, that is "mine own" and at the same time is "not mine own." If I can let it show itself and withdraw, let it be my own and not my own, if I can be open to the mystery, then I can live in the circle of loving and knowing, I can breathe the high mountain air of the love of God.

I get stuck at this point, though, if I can't get beyond the thought of what is mine. There is a release in saying "Mine own, and not mine own," if I can say it meaning "Yes." I release all I love and am released by all I love. An element of detachment comes into my love. What I am thinking, nevertheless, when I say "Yes" is not just release, not just willingness but also hope. I can say "Mine own, and not mine own" with simple resignation, with simple willingness, with "infinite resignation" as Kierkegaard says, taking into account the mystery that shows itself here and at the same time withdraws. Or I can say it with "faith," as he describes it, a paradoxical combination of willingness and hope, a willingness that is a letting be and a hope that is an openness to the mystery. The willingness is the recognition and acceptance of the gift that is "Mine own, and not mine own." The hope is that the love offered to me in this elusive gift, as I live in its radiance, a sun rising and setting in a world "full of gentle suffering and mysterious grace,"[11] will be enough for me, will fulfill my heart's desire.

"Infinite resignation expresses the recognition and acceptance of God's love," Barbara Anderson comments. "But faith is our finite repetition of God's love for us."[12] Infinite resignation is my recognition and acceptance of the divine love that is expressed in the human beings, my loved ones, who are "Mine own, and not mine own." It is infinite because of the divine love I see expressed in them, but it is resignation because I could have wished them to be simply "Mine own." And faith is my finite repetition of God's love for me, my own living and loving, following love's direction. "The future— any future," Patricia McKillip says in a story, "is simply one step at a time out of the heart,"[13] and living by faith is that, living one step at a time out of the heart.

If we love with a love we know, then infinite resignation is the highest wisdom, and its expression is "Mine own, and not mine own." But if we love with a love we do not know, as Aquinas seemed to say in my dream, then the highest wisdom is faith and we don't know where faith will take us, living one step at a time out of the heart. Quiet eyes become "the eyes of faith,"[14] and the mystery that shows itself and at the same time withdrawn in "Mine own, and not mine own" draws us on into the unknown. "Unless one hopes," Heraclitus said, "one will not find the unhoped-for."[15] I don't know what to hope for beyond "Mine own, and not mine own," but by hoping nonetheless I open myself to the mystery of the unhoped-for, and by living one step at a time out of the heart, I enter one step at a time into the mystery, I find the unhoped-for. I find myself walking on "the road of the union of love with God."[16]

The Friends of God

"guided and guarded"
— J. R. R. Tolkien

"As God is one," Newman says, "so the impression which He gives us of Himself is one."[1] It is an impression of presence, of "I am with you," of companionship on the journey of life. It is the impression we have when something touches the deep loneliness in us, when "heart speaks to heart," as Newman says, when music is "from the heart," as Beethoven says, "may it go to the heart."[2] Then it seems we are not alone. Then it seems God is with us. Our life is a journey in time and God is our companion on the way.

There are times, though, when the impression of presence is not there, when it seems therefore God is not there. We go through something we didn't think God would allow, a testing of the heart, the kind of thing we pray against, "And lead us not into temptation, but deliver us from evil." Then it can seem we have encountered another side of God, a side turned away from us like the other side of the moon. If we hold to God nonetheless, we come to realize it is not another side of God we are experiencing so much as the essential ordeal of a journey with God. Every journey has its ordeal, according to storytelling, an ordeal by fire, by water, by sheer endurance, and a journey with God has its ordeal too, the ordeal of the human heart, the trial where the secrets of the heart are revealed. If I come upon that ordeal, I may find that my heart is divided, that it is not entirely with God. Still, I do not thereby fail the test. For I can bring my divided heart to God to be made whole. I can bring all my heart to God, although it is a heart in pieces, a broken heart.

9

If I may take my own ordeals of the heart as "the dealings of Wisdom with the elect soul,"[3] as Newman describes them, then I can still think of myself as a friend of God, "guided and guarded" even when I seem left to myself. If God leads us by the heart, then even the testing of the heart, when we seem left to ourselves, is a guiding, for the revealing of the secrets of the heart, the revealing that my heart is divided, for instance, is a showing of the way. I am shown that my heart is divided and that I am called to wholeness. There is also a guarding in this being left to myself. "His grief he will not forget," Tolkien says, "but it will not darken his heart, it will teach him wisdom."[4] I am guarded from a darkening of the heart, and I am guided, being taught wisdom, the wisdom of love, of loving with all my heart, and with all my soul, and with all my mind, and with all my strength.

Once a friend of mine told me, "You see life as a journey with God, but I see it as a wrestling with God." Now, many years later, I still see life as a journey with God, but I see my friend's vision of a conflict with God better than I did. The vision of a journey with God, I think, is that of a friend of God; that of a wrestling with God is perhaps the vision of a lover of God—I think of the conflicts of love. The test of loneliness may be a crisis on the way from being a friend to being a lover. I sometimes think our whole civilization has been going through such a crisis, "that the thoughts of many hearts may be revealed."[5]

A Guiding Presence

"He was guided and guarded,"[6] a storyteller like Tolkien can say, counting on what Walter Benjamin calls "the ability to exchange experiences."[7] For if we can exchange experiences with each other we can learn from one another's experience, we can "counsel and be counseled," as Benjamin puts it. What is more, we can learn from our own experience, we can be "guided." "A man is receptive to counsel only to the extent that he allows his situation to speak,"

Benjamin says. That is what it is to be guided, to allow one's situation to speak. We can come to a point, however, where we no longer allow our situation to speak and where we ourselves fall silent. "Was it not noticeable at the end of the war that men returned from the battlefield grown silent— not richer but poorer in communicable experience?" Benjamin asks, speaking of the First World War. Something had happened, he thought, that seemed to refute our experience and to silence our storytelling. "It is as if something that seemed inalienable to us, the securest among our possessions were taken away from us," he says, "the ability to exchange experiences."

Everything depends on our ability to exchange experiences, it seems, the guiding, the guarding, the sense of presence. Or it depends, I should say, on our *willingness* to exchange experiences. "He was guided and guarded," Tolkien says of a traveler who has a star shining from his forehead but who, according to the story, has finally to hand on the star to another—the guiding and guarding he receives is a gift he cannot keep for himself. So it is too with the guiding and guarding we receive with our experience. When something terrible happens to us against our will, however, something that contradicts our experience, we may be unwilling to share it, unwilling to acknowledge it, because we are unwilling, even after the fact, to have undergone it at all. It remains separate from our experience, therefore, and a kind of numbing sets in, and we grow silent.

What corresponds to the star shining from the forehead in our experience is the love of God, for it is the love of One whose love cannot be limited to oneself alone. It is a guiding principle, if I act on love, and a guarding principle, if I abide in love. And it is something I cannot keep for myself. Satan's fall, according to one view (that of Al-Hallaj), was due to jealous love, wanting God's love for himself alone. When something happens to me that seems contrary to the love of God, however, then all the guiding and guarding I have known seems contradicted. "After all, counsel is less an answer to a question than a proposal concerning the continuation of a story which is just unfolding," Walter Benjamin says. "To seek this counsel one would first have to be able to tell the story."[8] When something happens that seems contrary to the love of God, it seems contrary also to the story I have known. I seem to be in a different story than I had imagined. To be able to tell the story now I have to become willing to have undergone what has happened, I have to be able to believe the love of God is present where it seems to be absent. Only then can I begin to understand "the continuation of a story which is just unfolding."

As a guiding principle, love is a direction I bring to each situation in which I find myself. "Love is a direction," Simone Weil says, "and not a state of soul."[9] The direction can be there, she is saying, without us feeling the presence of God. It must make a difference, though, if we do feel the love, if we do feel the presence. What difference does it make? Indeed let us ask the question *What difference does love's direction make?*

There is a direction already in the situation to which we bring love, "time's arrow" from the past to the future. In bringing the love of God to the situations or finding it in them, we are turning time's arrow into love's direction, seeing everyone and everything not just coming from the past and going to the future but coming from God and going to God. We are turning the straight arrow into a circle. We are discovering the curvature of time. I think of Augustine in his *Confessions*, seeing his own story and that of the whole world as "the story of the soul wandering away from God and then in torment and tears finding its way home."[10] I think of the four cycles of storytelling: (1) once all things were at one and we could understand the language of other living beings, (2) then the human race emerged and separated from all else, (3) now the individual has emerged and separated from humanity, and (4) one day we will all be one again with each other and with God. As it is now, the time of the emerged individual, "the solitary individual," as Benjamin says, who is "uncounseled and cannot counsel others,"[11] the rest of the story, especially its beginning in primordial unity and its ending in universal reunion, can seem merely story and not at all reality.

Storytelling, according to Walter Benjamin, is something we are leaving behind us, something that is receding into the distance in time. If I am not mistaken about the cycles of story, though, we are living in one cycle, that of the emergence and separation of the individual, and are on our way into another, that of the reunion with humanity and with God. The storytelling that is receding into the distance is that of the earlier cycles. We are going through the test of loneliness meanwhile that belongs to the separation of the individual from humanity. That is why it seems we are "solitary" and "uncounseled" and "cannot counsel others." And as the cycle ends for us and the cycle of reunion begins, we have the experience of having thought we were living in one story only to discover with new hope and apprehension that we are living in another.

Say I find myself at the turning point, at the point of transition described in the classical "rules for the discernment of spirits,"[12] where I am passing from outer to inner influences, where the spiritual influences I can discern, that is, are no longer just the outer but also the inner. Autonomy and self-sufficiency, the endpoint of the individual's emergence and separation, look possible only so long as all influences seem to be from the outside. When they appear to be from the inside as well, then I know I am not alone, I know I am on my way to reunion with God and with humanity. Say I come to a crisis of outer influences by becoming involved in a destructive relationship with another person, a relationship I mean where there is a seeking for love but there is no love. I am seeking love from another and the other is seeking love from me, but we do not love one another. What comes to light in such an experience is my weakest point, and that weakest point becomes the turning point. For it is my self-insufficiency, my need and my need to be needed, that leaves me open to destructive situations. Up until now I have had a sense of God's presence only when something happens to meet my need and my need to be needed, to make me feel unalone. Now I find there are times when God seems present anyway, when God is with me even in the midst of my loneliness.

I go from feeling abandoned by God in destructive situations, that is, to realizing God has been there all along. "We all have within us a center of stillness surrounded by silence,"[13] Dag Hammarskjöld says. "We all" suggests that we are connected with one another even when we are alone; "surrounded by silence" suggests God is present even when God seems absent. For there are times when I am in my center of stillness and am surrounded by a silence that speaks, that sings to the heart. I am aware then not just of the present but of presence in the present, and yet there is nothing happening outside of me to make me feel unalone. When the silence does not speak, on the other hand, when it does not sing to the heart, I am still aware of the silence itself, still aware of being surrounded by it. If the silence is the presence, then I live in the presence, even when it does not speak, even when it does not sing.

At the turning point between personal emergence and universal reunion, therefore, I enter into my own center of stillness to find God and to find the rest of humanity. I pass really from time to eternity, from the bare present to presence in the present, from a present that consists of "information" that "does not survive the moment in which it is new," as Walter Benjamin says, to a presence in the present that "does not expend itself" but like a story "preserves and concentrates its strength and is capable of releasing it even after a long time."[14] What I am ascribing to the presence, Benjamin is ascribing to the story, for the story bears the mark of the presence, the mark of "eternity," as he puts it, in "the slow piling one on top of the other of thin transparent layers" of "a variety of retellings."[15] If we think of time as "a changing image of eternity," Plato's description, then eternity shines through "the slow piling one on top of the other of thin transparent layers" of time. Instead of saying with Benjamin "the time is past in which time did not matter," accordingly, I want to say time still conveys the presence of eternity.

Time began to matter for us with the emergence of humanity and our separation from the primordial unity of all beings. It began to matter for each of us with the emergence of the person and the separation of the individual person from humanity. Eternity, however, is not just something that recedes into the past the more we get away from the primordial unity, nor is it just something that gets closer the more we approach the universal reunion. It is not just "the time when time did not matter." It is rather a timeless presence in time. Our journey in time, I want to say, is not just from God and towards God but is also with God. "Love is of such a nature that it changes us into the things we love,"[16] Meister Eckhart says. That is how I want to interpret "the slow piling one on top of the other of thin transparent layers" of time. Love is changing us over time into the things we love.

When we try to discern love's direction, we have to consider the things we love and how we are being changed into them over time. If the change is like thin transparent layers of lacquer, then it is essentially an enhancement of what we already are. Or, if it is like the retellings of a story, an enhancement of what has already happened or of what has already been told. Sometimes, however, "I'm outside my heart, looking for the way back in."[17] I am out of touch with the things I love, "outside my heart," seeking for love's direction, "looking for the way back in." Then I have to discern whether I have taken a wrong turn or whether I am indeed on the way but have simply lost sight of it ahead. One thought that may come is that of a person I have loved and lost. Does love's direction take me back to the loved one I have lost? No, not necessarily, if the phrase "the things we love" may be taken as a guide. "What are the things I love?" I have to ask myself. "Life and light and love," I may answer, borrowing the terms of the Gospel of John. If love changes us into the things we love, then by loving life I may come to life, by loving light I may come to light, by loving love I may come to love. Coming to life and light and love is an enhancement of what I am, of what has happened, of what has been told in my story. It is the opposite of being "bereft" of life and light and love, and yet not the opposite of being "bereaved" of a loved one.

If I am outside my heart, looking for the way back in, I think at first of the life I have not lived, of the road I have not taken, and I feel a bereavement, but then I think of the dream I have had that is still to be fulfilled, the dream of being a friend of God, and I think of "the road of the union of love with God,"[18] the road, I believe, of the heart's desire, and how even now I can be walking that road. There is "only one Road," if you are thinking this way, "like a great river," as Tolkien says, "its springs at every doorstep, and every path its tributary."[19] And the very next step I take, thinking of this road and intending to walk it, I find myself again inside my heart. The way back in is the "one Road." "You step into the Road," Tolkien says, "and if you don't keep your feet, there is no knowing where you might be swept off to." You are carried back into your heart and carried forward by your heart.

"Boredom is the dream bird that hatches the egg of experience,"[20] Benjamin says, thinking of the time when time does not matter, the time of storytelling. Boredom, though, is a craving for excitement, and it can lead one to step into the road not taken seeking adventure, or it can lead one instead to step into "the road of the union of love with God," following the heart. The craving for excitement is not the same as the heart's desire, is encompassed by it rather, for the heart seeks peace and not just adventure. The time of storytelling, the time when time does not matter, "hatches the egg of experience," gives shape to my experience, by enabling me to see myself living in a story that is still going on. It makes a difference, though, if I only imagine taking a road I have not taken in life, living a life I have not lived, or if instead I see myself actually taking the road of the heart's desire, living my life to the full. It is the difference between the feeling of boredom where time is in endless supply and that of an unending story where, as Tolkien says, "the road goes ever on and on."

Boredom makes you want "to go as far as possible—to the end of yourself," as Kenneth White says in *The Blue Road*, speaking of his journey to Labrador, "till you get into a territory where time turns into space, where things appear in all their nakedness and the wind blows anonymously."[21] Heart's desire leads into adventure too, and it can be hard to tell whether the road ahead I am contemplating is really that "of the union of love with God." The main touchstone is the peace the heart seeks, where instead of time turning into space there is timeless presence in time. If I am outside my heart, looking for the way back in, and I find myself inside my heart again as soon as I step into the road, then I can be confident it is the true road. It is no occasion on the road that gives me comfort, no meeting for instance, just the road itself, the sense of being led by the heart, of being led by God.

If I do then go on to meet someone on the road, someone I have loved or someone I come to love, I can think of it as more than a chance meeting. I can think of the other as belonging to my life, belonging to my way. "You may find friends upon your way when you least look for it,"[22] Tolkien says. These friends belong not just to my emergence as an individual, I realize at this turning point where I am, but to my reunion with humanity and with God. I do not leave them behind me, therefore, to reach autonomy, but our friendship can be enduring. "To go as far as possible—to the end of yourself" is to go to the endpoint of emergence and separation. That is "where time turns into space, where things appear in all their nakedness and the wind blows anonymously." It is where I become autonomous, as if I were Adam, the first and as yet the only human being, giving all things their names. To make the turn to reunion, though, is to go beyond "the end of yourself," to step into a road that "goes ever on and on" as other human paths join it, as it leads on and on into the union of love.

Time turning into space, history giving way to geography, as it can when you are traveling in wild and unsettled territory, is a freeing from the past, an opening to the future, the essence of personal autonomy. Timeless presence in time, on the other hand, is a light guiding you from the past into the future, as in Newman's prayer "Lead, kindly light," leading one step at a time, as a presence must lead, always illuminating a present. "I do not ask to see the distant scene," he prays, "one step enough for me."[23] The presence is felt as a peace, changing the inevitable arrow of time past and future into something willing, a "Thanks!" for the past, a "Yes!" to the future. The love of God, if I am on the right track here, is like a great river in which we are all caught up. It is the very river of time. Yet it is one thing to know the river is time and another to know it is love.

If the river is simply time, then with the lapse of time everything is passing away. If the river is love, however, and "love is of such a nature that it changes us into the things we love," then none of the things we love is lost. Naming the things I love, I said "life and light and love," using the terms of the Gospel of John. I might have said instead "hope and peace and friends and intelligence." Anyway the things I am naming are not simply situations of life but they have to do, rather, with my relationship to the situations. It is the relationship that is lasting even while the situations are passing. But what of the situations themselves? They live in memory and can come to life again when they are remembered. What is more, they bring to life in being remembered the person I was, uniting him with the person I am. "A minute freed from the order of time has recreated in us, to feel it, the man freed from the order of time,"[24] Marcel Proust says in *Remembrance of Things Past*. It is this person "freed from the order of time" who is capable of "life and light and love," of "hope and peace and friends and intelligence." It is this person who can say "I am."

"And one can understand that this man should have confidence in his joy," Proust continues, ". . . one can understand that the word 'death' should have no meaning for him; situated outside time, why should he fear the future?" Being "outside time," I take it, is not the same as being "outside my heart." I recall Martin Versfeld once remarking that Augustine in his *Confessions* "was having the time of his life." Remembering the things of his past, Augustine was reliving the whole time of his life, thus literally "having the time of his life," and he was also feeling "confidence in his joy" and thus figuratively too "having the time of his life." That confidence in joy, though, seems to require going like Augustine from memory to understanding to will, not just remembering the situations of my past but allowing them to speak and responding with the "Thanks!" of my will and the "Yes!" that takes away my fear of death and the future.

"Thanks!" (the overcoming of regret), and "Yes!" (the overcoming of fear) are not possible, it seems, without an understanding of the past that enables me to see my way into the future. Augustine's understanding was that God was with him even when he was wandering away from God and not only when he was finding his way home to God with tears. His tears of sorrow for sin are compatible with the joy of his thanksgiving, his confession of sin with his confession of praise. He is able "to cast aside regret and fear" and "to do the deed at hand." I need a similar understanding of my past, I think, to see my way into the future, an understanding that God was with me even when I seemed left to myself and not only when I was touched with the sense of God's presence. "Counsel woven into the fabric of real life is wisdom,"[25] Walter Benjamin says. It is counsel offered by the sage in Tolkien's story "to cast aside regret and fear" and "to do the deed at hand."[26] It is wisdom, woven into the fabric of real life, to understand that God was with me even when I seemed left to myself, that God was always with me and is with me still.

It is wisdom, "the epic side of truth," as Benjamin says, and it places me in an epic, a journey with God in time where "the road goes ever on and on" because the journey is God's own journey. But what of the other side of truth that my friend spoke of, life as a conflict rather than a journey with God? If the will of God and our heart's desire were at odds, then life would indeed be a wrestling with God. I want rather to say the will of God and our own deepest heart's desire are one,

"his will is our peace," as is said in Dante's *Paradiso,* but is this
only "a way of avoiding the real of desire"?[27] Certainly there
is much in life that is opposed to "our peace." I want to say it
is also opposed to "his will." I think of destructive situations
in life, of human relations that are destructive. If I say they
are opposed to God's will, I have to say God works against
them, guards against them. But if God is against them, how
do they ever occur?

A Guarding Presence

Love's direction guards us not against grief but against a
darkening of the heart. I am taking Tolkien's remark as my
guide here, "His grief he will not forget, but it will not darken
his heart, it will teach him wisdom." For love can make me
vulnerable to grief and suffering. When I love someone or
something, when I care, I am exposed to sorrow, I can suffer
the loss of that person, of that thing that is so dear to me,
I can come to grief I would never feel if I did not love,
if I did not care. But if I abide in love, even in my grief,
I can learn the wisdom that comes of suffering instead of
succumbing to the darkness that can also come upon the
heart from suffering. The wisdom, the light, is that of love.
"There are places in the heart which do not yet exist," as
Leon Bloy says, "and into them enters suffering that they
may have existence."[28] The wisdom is the light that comes of
new depths and dimensions of feelings. The darkness is that
of lovelessness, the loss of light and feeling, the numbing of
the heart. If I abide in love, I come to new feeling. If I do
not abide in love, I lose even the feeling I have.

Imagination is also darkened. "But let us not darken our
hearts by imagining the trial of their gentle loyalty in the
Dark Tower,"[29] Tolkien has in another place. The imagination of the heart can be darkened by the horror and the fascination of torment, if one yields to the horror, if one yields to
the fascination, and allows it to captivate one's imagination.
There is "a choice of nightmare"[30] here, as Joseph Conrad

calls it in *Heart of Darkness*. There is a nightmare of soul in the darkening of the imagination of the heart by horror and fascination, and there is a nightmare of soullessness in the numbing of the heart and the loss of feeling. Still, one is confronted with the choice, I believe, only if one does not open one's heart to the light, to the wisdom that comes of suffering.

Abiding in love, if love is a direction and not a state of soul, means holding to the direction rather than to the feeling of love. "Do not seek death. Death will find you," Dag Hammarskjöld tells himself in *Markings*. "But seek the road which makes death a fulfillment."[31] "Do not seek love. Love will find you," I tell myself in a somewhat similar vein. "But seek the road of the union of love with God." Do not seek the feeling, I am saying to myself, the feeling will come to you. But seek the direction of love. There is a profound link here between love and death, between the road of love and "the road which makes death a fulfillment." If the direction of love can be there without the feeling, then it can be hard to discern between "the night of the spirit," as it is called, and the nightmare of soullessness that comes of abandoning the direction of love. So too, if the horror and the fascination can come over one's imagination without one succumbing to it, then it can be hard to discern between "the night of sense," as it is called, and the nightmare of soul that comes of succumbing to horror and fascination.

It is the road of love that makes the difference, "the road which makes death a fulfillment." The night of the soul falls upon the road; the nightmare of soul and of soullessness comes of abandoning the road. It is love that makes death a fulfillment. Instead of being simply the end of a loveless life, death is the consummation of love. As Walter Benjamin says, "a sequence of images is set in motion inside a man as his life comes to an end—unfolding views of himself under which he has encountered himself without being aware of it," and "suddenly in his expression and looks the unforgettable emerges."[32] What is the unforgettable?

Inscape, I would say, the inwardness of a life, of a person, that comes through in telling the life story. At death "the unforgettable emerges," Benjamin says, "and imparts to everything that concerned him that authority which even the poorest wretch in dying possesses for the living around him." Say I see myself as having been "guided and guarded." Say I see my life in terms of "the discernment of spirits" or of "spiritual influences," not that I have always followed the good and rejected the evil, but that my life has been a battleground of good and evil influences, thus a conflict, and yet has been guided and guarded, thus a journey. What emerges is the road I have traveled along with the many encounters that have taken place on the road, "a sequence of images" therefore "unfolding views" of myself under which I have "encountered" myself "without being aware of it." Whenever my life opens up before me all the way to death, whenever I encounter a *memento mori,* a reminder of my mortality, I have this experience, very like that in the actual hour of death. It is a moment when inscape becomes insight and I know my heart.

At times I have walked in the light, I can see, and at times I have walked in darkness. I see nevertheless that God has been with me even in the dark. To see that resolves the nightmare into the night, even if it is the night Christ speaks of in the Gospel of John when he says "Night cometh."[33] What has changed is not the past itself but my relationship with the past and consequently my relationship also with the future. My nightmare of soul becomes my night of sense, and my nightmare of soullessness becomes my night of the spirit, a purification of sense and spirit, as I awaken from the nightmare, as I learn "purity of heart is to will one thing."

"Our life is no dream," Novalis says, "but it should and perhaps will become one"[34] to us when we awaken from it. George MacDonald quotes this saying at the end of his first fantasy novel, *Phantastes,* where he describes a nightmare of soul, and also at the end of his last, *Lilith,* where he describes a nightmare of soullessness, and in both of them the saying, as he takes it, alludes to an awakening to purity of heart. One *awakens* to purity of heart, to the willing of one thing. It is an awakening that occurs at death but also at the encounters with death that take place during life. I awaken again and again in life, from the nightmare of soul and of soullessness, to discover the true desire of my heart. But then again and again I fall asleep, and again I dream, and once more I am caught up in the nightmare of horror and fascination and in the deeper nightmare of a loveless life, unloving, unloved, unlovely. The awakening, whenever it occurs, is a kindling of the heart that undoes the effects of spiritual numbing, an illumining that dissipates horror and fascination, an awakening that reveals the heart's desire.

This "again and again" quality of falling asleep and waking up can make the theme of willing one thing seem a repetitious one. "Is genius therefore so slow?" exclaims Albert Camus reading *Purity of Heart Is to Will One Thing* by Søren Kierkegaard. "Purity of heart for Kierkegaard is unity," Camus goes on to say. "But it is unity *and* the good. There is no purity outside of God. Conclusion: resign oneself to the impure? I am far from the good and I thirst for unity. That is irreparable."[35] The answer, I think, is that purity of heart is not an achievement but something that we awaken to, something that is already there. God is the heart's desire, I mean, but the heart doesn't know that until it awakens.

"My soul was not still enough for songs," MacDonald says in *Phantastes*. "Only in the silence and darkness of the soul's night do those stars of the inward firmament sink to its lower surface from the singing realms beyond, and shine upon the conscious spirit."[36] As long as I am caught up in the imagination of my heart, in the dread and fascination that are the nightmare of the soul, my soul is not still enough for songs, not still enough for purity of heart, for willing one thing. I am like MacDonald himself in the story, falling prey to the dread and to the fascination and then feeling remorse afterwards at my own weakness. It is the story of his adventures in the wonderland of imagination. He wanders in a dream that becomes at times a nightmare, meeting good and evil figures, a figure of dread and horror such as the spirit of the ash tree, a figure of fascination and seduction such as the spirit of the alder tree, a helping figure such as the wise old woman in the cottage, a figure needing help such as the beautiful woman imprisoned in marble. So too I meet people in waking life whom I invest with the power of my imagination, with my dread and my fascination, with helping power and with the need of my help.

"My spirits rose as I went deeper into the forest; but I could not regain my former elasticity of mind," he says. "I found cheerfulness to be like life itself—not to be created by any argument."[37] This after falling prey to fascination and seduction. "Afterwards I learned, that the best way to manage some kinds of painful thoughts, is to dare them to do their worst," he continues; "to let them lie and gnaw at your heart till they are tired; and you find you still have a residue of life they cannot kill." When I fall prey to the dread or to the fascination with which I have invested persons of my life, I have a feeling of moral failure, and I cannot seem to regain my joy. But then if I let these painful thoughts of failure lie and gnaw at my heart till they are tired, I find I still have a residue of life they cannot kill, something indestructible in me out of which "hope springs eternal" and joy too springs eternal.

What I am doing is letting my nightmare of dread and fascination become a purifying "night of sense" in which I go from living in the imagination of my heart to living clear down in my heart. Saint John of the Cross in *Dark Night of the Soul* describes the night of sense mainly as a time of spiritual dryness, sense finding no fulfillment in things of the spirit, and that indeed is what I find when I come to live in my heart, a spiritual desolation where hope and joy spring up like an unexpected oasis. Yet he does mention "formidable trials and temptations of sense" occurring in this time that seem to correspond to what I am calling the "nightmare of soul" and describing in terms of dread and fascination. "As a rule," he says, "these storms and trials are sent by God in this night and purgation of sense to those whom afterwards He purposes to lead into the other night,"[38] the night of the spirit. As I understand it, I come here into "the silence and darkness of the soul's night" and "those stars of the inward firmament sink to its lower surface" and "shine upon the conscious spirit" and my soul becomes "still enough for songs."

Imagination is still there, when I go from living in my imagination to living in my heart, but imagination becomes still enough and empty enough to compose songs. It becomes like the starting point of creation when "the earth was without form and void, and darkness was upon the face of the deep, and the Spirit of God was moving over the face of the waters."[39] Imagination, I sometimes think, is my strength and my weakness. Certainly it is a strength and a weakness, and what is happening here as I go from living in imagination to living in the heart is that I am going from imagination as a weakness, where I am prey to dread and fascination, to imagination as a strength, where I am "still enough for songs." When I come to live in my heart, however, I encounter my own unkindled heart, my lovelessness, and thus I enter into "the night of the spirit."

A slow kindling of the heart, a slow passage from lovelessness to love, is the story MacDonald tells in *Lilith*. It is the story of his journey through a looking glass to meet his own soul and his own death. He goes from books to people, beginning in his library where at first he cares only about books but where he enters nonetheless into another world, comes to feel his loneliness and meets his own soul in the form of Lilith, the first wife of Adam according to legend. He finds her withered and nearly dead, and she is not redeemed until at last she is able to weep. Again and again he is faced with his own death in the story and is asked to accept it as a way to life. After twice refusing, he finally accepts. It is a story I recognize in my own experience. "Work as an anesthetic against loneliness, books as a substitute for people!" Dag Hammarskjöld says to himself in his diary. "You say you are waiting, that the door stands open. For what? People? Is not the Etna for which Empedocles is waiting, a fate beyond human companionship?"[40] The solution, as in

MacDonald's story, turns out to be the acceptance of death, "Thanks!" and "Yes!" That is the kindling of the heart, the passing from lovelessness to love.

I cannot have love without death; I cannot have death without love. Those who will not die cannot get through loneliness, according to MacDonald's story, and those who will not love cannot get through death. Why? One of Lilith's hands is closed in the story. She cannot love, she cannot die, until she opens her hand. That is how it is with me. I cannot love, I cannot die, until I open my hand. Death is a letting go of everyone and everything, and so is love, if it is the love of God, a letting go of everyone and everything to enter into a new relation with everyone and everything, to be whole, to be heart and soul in relationship with everyone and everything. The hand is closed on someone or something I am holding on to. If I open it, I let go of whoever or whatever I am keeping back.

I come to the point where I have "extreme spiritual sensitiveness but no spiritual faith in life," as Turner says in his essay on Mozart; I come to the point where "some affirmation of the soul is inexorably demanded."[41] Lilith is able to weep but is not yet able to open her hand. My "Thanks!" and my "Yes!" is that act of faith, that affirmation of the soul, that opening of my hand. Before I come to make that act of thanksgiving and of affirmation, I am capable of "mental poise," even of "invariable serenity and good temper" in Turner's words, but it is a surface "beneath which is a fathomless black water," "an abyss of black melancholy," a "quiet hopelessness," altogether compatible nevertheless with a "sense of humor" and a "sense of spiritual life." What is still lacking is a "quiet, steady, flaming faith," the simple and sublime faith of those who "walked with God." And that is what I come to at last in uttering my "Thanks!" for the past and my "Yes!" to the future, uttering it in hope, in trust that heart's desire will come true, though I do not see how it will or even how it could. I simply put my hand, now opened, in God's.

"Faith is the marriage of God and the soul,"[42] Dag Hammarskjöld writes in his diary, quoting Saint John of the Cross, soon after uttering his own "Thanks!" and "Yes!" That is what I am coming to, I think, putting my hand in God's, a marriage of God and the soul, something very simple, almost too simple to describe, walking with God, living in spiritual faith. Perhaps this is what Kierkegaard was talking about when he said "Purity of heart is to will one thing." If I describe it this way, though, I realize right away that the simplicity is not attained once and for all. I have to return to it again and again after having wasted my spirit, after having wasted my time and my strength, after having fallen away from the one to the many. I have to wake up again and again, morning after morning, as it were, after having fallen asleep.

I have to say "Thanks!" again after things have happened to me that I did not think God would allow, "Yes!" again after things have become more uncertain therefore than they were. Each repetition, however, carries me further along the road of the union of love with God. The wheel turns round and round, but the vehicle is moving forward. "Such are the dealings of Wisdom with the elect soul," I want to say with Newman. "She will bring upon him fear, and dread, and trial; and She will torture him with the tribulation of Her discipline, till She try him by Her laws, and trust his soul," he quotes from the Wisdom of Sirach. "Then she will strengthen him, and make her way straight to him, and give him joy."[43] Perhaps I may envision the marriage of God and the soul as it is in The Wisdom of Solomon, a marriage with the figure of Wisdom.[44] When she strengthens me, and makes her way straight to me, and gives me joy, then my "Thanks!" and "Yes!" which were so hard to utter become easy, and love's direction becomes clear. *As time's arrow becomes love's direction, time becomes transparent to eternity, becomes a changing image of eternity.*

"Time can become constitutive only when connection with the transcendental home has been lost,"[45] Walter Benjamin says, quoting Georg Lukacs. What I am doing when I say "Thanks!" for the past and "Yes!" to the future is regaining connection with the transcendental home. It is true, the actual saying of "Thanks!" and "Yes!" is simply an expression of the orientation, love's direction, already present. To say time's arrow *becomes* love's direction is to say it comes to expression and thus to realization. The connection seems lost when the emerged individual stands over and against time, when I face my death. But when I accept my death, when I say "Yes!" I no longer stand over and against it, and time becomes transparent, becomes, as it is indeed, a changing image of eternity. I think of moments in Mozart's music, for instance his "Ave Verum" written in his last year, where he sings serenely of the hour of death.

Or there is a dramatic suspension, I should say, when he comes to the words about death, *in mortis examine*, then a harmonic resolution as he repeats them and comes to peace and repose. It is as in life, there is a suspension whenever I face my own death, then a resolution as I accept it and come again to repose in life. I am not able to walk with God as long as I am standing over and against death, but when I accept it, God is there at my side. It is the same when things happen I did not think God would allow. As long as I am standing over and against my life, I am not able to walk with God, but as soon as I accept my life, God is there at my side. It is like proving the existence of God. As long as I hold on to the proof, the existence of God eludes me, as Kierkegaard says,[46] but as soon as I let go of the proof, the existence of God is there. When I stand over and against my own death, over and against my own life, it is as if I were seeking some evidence, some testimony, some proof of God. When I accept my death, when I accept my life, I align myself with God, my will with God's will, and God is my companion on the way.

So when I think my friendship with God is at an end because of what has happened, or was never there in the first place or was only an illusion, I find hope and peace and friendship and understanding once again as I align my will with God's, as I verify those words of Dante that Matthew Arnold thought were the greatest in all poetry, "his will is our peace." The union of love with God is a matter of memory, of understanding, of will being taken up with God, according to Saint Teresa of Avila,[47] but especially of will. It is a matter of will becoming willingness. The union is essentially a union of wills, the human will and the divine. As I align my will with God's, I come to a transfiguration of memory in my "Thanks!" and a transfiguration of understanding in my "Yes!" I come to stand in a simple vision of all coming from God and going to God, a vision of home in God, of God with us in homecoming.

There is "a spiritual sublimity which surpasses in value all other human emotions, and which only the few supreme spirits of this earth have ever expressed," Turner says in his essay on Mozart. "At present it is the rare emotional possession of the few, but nothing can prevent its slowly dominating mankind. Its power is irresistible because it is latent in us all."[48] I believe it is "a direction, not a state of soul," it is love's direction, but when it is felt, when it does become a state of soul, it is indeed a spiritual sublimity surpassing all other human emotions. It is latent in us all, I believe too, as a direction, latent in the form of the heart's longing, and it comes to ascendancy in our lives when we go with it, when we affirm it or confirm it with our will. Yet as will and heart's desire are not one and the same, are not necessarily in accord, heart's desire is not irresistible and its ascendancy is not inevitable. Everything depends on us going with it willingly, on abandon, as it were, abandon of the human will to the divine will. It is in moments of abandon to the love of God that we come to the heights of the human spirit.

The Words and the Music

"First the music,
then the words"
— Antonio Salieri

There is a way of words and a way of music, and it can happen that you feel compelled to choose at some point between the words and the music. So it was for me. I felt compelled to choose between the words and the music as the devotion of my life. I chose the words. But now, after many years and many words, I feel able to return to music. And, even as I write this, I am also working on a song cycle, writing the words and composing the music. It can happen thus, after some lapse of time, that the two ways rejoin, and you are able to take "the road not taken" without having thereby to abandon the road you have already taken in life.

As the devotion of a life, the way of words, of knowing and loving words, is a way to the essence of things, and to the essence of knowing too, and to the essence of loving. And yet in reading "We feel quite truly that our wisdom begins where that of the author ends, and we would like to have him give us answers, while all he can do is give us desires," as Marcel Proust says in his essay *On Reading*. "And these desires he can arouse in us only by making us contemplate the supreme beauty which the last effort of his art has permitted him to reach."[1] There is a kindling of the heart, an illumining of the mind. Our reading kindles our desires, it opens our eyes, but it always leaves us unfulfilled, always points beyond itself. Likewise our writing can kindle the hearts of others, can illumine their minds by leading them to contemplate

31

the beauty we ourselves contemplate, but that beauty itself
always lies beyond. It is the beauty of the essence of things.
It is the beauty of knowing. It is the beauty of loving. It is
the simplicity Aquinas contemplates after talking about the
complexity of being and essence, the simplicity of God "the
first principle which is of infinite simplicity. . . in which be
the end and the consummation of this discourse."[2]

I think of Aquinas living the desire to know God, to see
God face to face, of him saying "Nothing, Lord, but you,"[3]
speaking of his heart's desire, and at the end of his life
saying "I can write no more, and all I have written seems
like straw" as he began to get a glimpse of the vision of God.
The quality of words that lends itself to music seems to be
this quality of pointing beyond themselves to the essence of
things, to knowing and to loving, even to God. At the same
time, this is the quality of words that lends itself to what is
now called "deconstruction." As words can be *construed* as
pointing beyond themselves, so too they can be *deconstrued*,
as it were, when they are considered simply in themselves
and of themselves and by themselves. Then the words and
the music cease, and what is beyond is surrounded by silence.

If we follow in words and music the direction into the
beyond, we find "desires," as Proust says, we find the heart's
desire, and we are led to "contemplate the supreme beauty"
that others have been able to reach in vision, but then we
come back to desires of our own, and those perhaps are the
"desires" Proust meant, we come to the heart's desire as we
experience it and to our own vision of beauty. Reading and
listening is passing over to others; writing and composing
is coming back to ourselves. Let us trace this direction in
words that lend themselves to music, this "pointing beyond
themselves," and see where it leads us. Let us see if it leads us,
as the mystical theologians say, "into the darkness with love."[4]

The Way of Words

There are "three voices of poetry," according to T. S. Eliot.
The first is the voice speaking for itself and to itself, only over-
heard, as it were, by others; the second is the voice addressing

an audience; and the third is the voice assuming the person of a character in a play. Consider the writing I am doing here, if this may be compared with poetry. I am speaking or writing in the second voice, addressing my readers. Yet I am also trying to pass over to others and to speak or write in the third voice, assuming the person of Proust, then the person of Aquinas, and now the person of Eliot. Then too I am reflecting on what I am doing here, speaking or writing to myself about it in the first voice, allowing others, as it were, to overhear me. "I think that in every poem, from the private meditation to the epic or the drama," Eliot says, "there is more than one voice to be heard."[5] It is in the voice that is heard, I want to say, that words point beyond themselves.

Consider therefore a more mysterious instance. The following sentences from Shakespeare are inscribed side by side on the stained glass windows of the Winchester House:

> Wide unclasp the tables of their thoughts;
> These same thoughts people this little world.[6]

In their original context these words are spoken in the third voice, the voice assuming the person of a character in a play. It is Ulysses in *Troilus and Cressida* who says "And wide unclasp the tables of their thoughts," describing "these encounterers" who do so. And it is Richard in *Richard II* who says "And these same thoughts people this little world," speaking of his own thoughts in his prison cell. But in the Winchester House the two verses combine and seem to be spoken in the second voice, the voice addressing an audience, here a voice addressing all those who come to the house.

Now suppose I write these words down in a diary, and then later quote them in a poem I write, a meditation of my own, spoken therefore in the first voice, the voice speaking for itself and to itself. The sentence "Wide unclasp the tables of their thoughts," a description when it was spoken in the third voice, became an exhortation or a command when spoken in the second, and now becomes for me a rule of life, a principle I am to observe in passing over to others. I am to "unclasp the tables of their thoughts," for "these same thoughts people this little world." By understanding the thoughts of others I am to understand the world or at least "this little world" of human beings. With the change of voice there has been a change of meaning, in the first sentence from the indicative to the imperative, in the second sentence from the little world of the prison cell to the little world of humanity. *Do the voices that are heard in poetry tell us of the essence of things?*

"There may be four voices," Eliot says. "There may be, perhaps, only two."[7] I want to include at least one other voice besides his three, namely that of the person before God, the voice calling out to God in prayer, as in the Psalms, as in the *Confessions* of Augustine. That may be essential to consider if we are to come to the essence of things. It is Proust who is especially known for speaking of "the essence of things" and for coming to it through "the remembrance of things past," Shakespeare's phrase, through the retrieval of time, Proust's own way of putting it in terms of "time lost" (*le temps perdu*) and "time found" (*le temps retrouvé*). Let us see if there is a link between the retrieval of time and the presence of eternity.

I can see how Proust is one of those who "wide unclasp the tables of their thoughts" in writing, and how "these same thoughts people this little world," the universe of his discourse. It is the tables of memory that he unclasps. What he comes to ultimately, as he says already in his little essay *On Reading*, is "the inviolate place of the Past" (*la place inviolable du Passé*), "of the Past familiarly risen in the midst of the present" (*du Passé familièrement surgi au milieu du présent*).[8] This inviolate place of the past, where the past exists in the present, where time does not lapse, is the place where the essence of things can be viewed. Say I reenact the process of recollection he describes in his essay, recollecting my own hours of reading in childhood, and let the memories linked with those hours come to mind. I find that the sequence of my readings is the sequence of my enthusiasms, the shapes that have been taken by my heart's desire. Not only the things of which I read come to mind, the adventures, the voyages and travels, the lives and times, but also the situations in which I read them, the rooms of home, the landscape and the night sky, the seascape of vacation, the inscape and the escape of my life, the thoughts and the world they peopled.

"There are perhaps no days of our childhood we lived so fully as those we believe we left without having lived them," Proust says, "those we spent with a favorite book."[9] As I trace the sequence of my enthusiasms as it appears in my readings, I find the stories that caught my imagination and I find the beginnings of my own story. It is as though I were trying to place my own story in the context of a larger story, like Geronimo beginning the narration of his own life with the Apache story of creation or Augustine ending the narration of his with the story of Genesis. "The universe is a series of leaping sparks," it has been said, "everything else is interpretation."[10] What interpretation, I ask myself, does my life bring to the leaping sparks? It is there, I expect, in my enthusiasms, in the successive shapes of my heart's desire.

A boundless desire to know is the desire I find expressed in the fairy tales a child learns, a desire "to survey the depths of space and time," as Tolkien says in his essay "On Fairy-Stories," a desire "to hold communion with other living things."[11] There is something else too, something that allows the child to seek knowledge so eagerly and confidently, a kind of trust that is the opposite of cynicism, the "basic trust" that is the task, according to Erik Erikson, of the earliest stage of life. It is a belief in the sincerity, the benevolence, the rectitude, the competence of others. Or since there are figures in stories who are insincere or malevolent or devious or unable to help, and since their contrast with the figures who are trustworthy is so marked and important an element of the tales, this basic trust becomes a belief in the ultimate triumph of sincerity and benevolence and rectitude and competence. Thus the happy ending is of the essence of the fairy tale, as Tolkien argues, and the happy ending hints at the vision of the universe that arises from faith, where "all shall be well, and all manner of thing shall be well."[12]

It only hints, though, for there is a change in hope as it passes from "basic trust" through all the chances of life to "faith," as Erikson describes it, "the last possible form of hope as matured."[13] Consider those words, "all shall be well, and all manner of thing shall be well," that T. S. Eliot quotes from Juliana of Norwich in his last poem "Little Gidding." Assuming the person of Juliana, he is speaking in the third voice of poetry, as he calls it, and is attempting to enter into her faith tried by suffering and illumined by visions. Speaking to us, he is speaking in the second voice, giving his last advice in his "farewell to poetry." Speaking to himself, he is speaking in the first voice, summoning up his own faith in the face of aging and death. Compare the last movement of Beethoven's last quartet, something Eliot seems to have in mind here, built on a little melody with the words[14]

Muss es sein?	Must it be?
Es muss sein!	It must be!
Es muss sein!	It must be!

Only when I come to a point in life beyond my child's vision, when I am faced with what Beethoven calls "the difficult (or really the heavy) resolution," *Der schwer gefasste Entschluss*, as he entitles this last movement, as if a light heart had become heavy, do I begin to understand those words, "Must it be? It must be! It must be!"[15] And it is only then that I understand those words of faith, as if a heavy heart had become light, "all shall be well, and all manner of thing shall be well." Coming to this point, my desire to know, "to survey the depths of space and time," "to hold communion with other living things," becomes a desire to know the thoughts of others, to "wide unclasp the tables of their thoughts," for "these same thoughts people this little world." My reading becomes a passing over into the thoughts, the lives, the times of others. The very things in his room, especially ones he had not chosen and were not useful to him, "peopled my room with thoughts somehow personal," Proust says, so that his room was "full to the brim with the soul of others."[16] So it is with my mind, as I continue to pass over into the soul of others and come back again to my own soul. Eventually my desire to know, as I come back to myself again and again, becomes a desire to know my own thoughts, to know what I can know, what I should do, what I may hope. It is then that I come to "the difficult resolution."

A desire to know, a desire to know the thoughts of others, then at last a desire to know my own thoughts, the "thoughts of the heart," *cogitationes cordis*, really to unburden my heart, those are the successive shapes of my desire. But that last shape takes me beyond my reading into my meditations and "the difficult resolution" of writing in the first voice of poetry, the solitary voice. It is possible to resolve issues of life in poetry, to give words, that is, to thoughts of the heart that have been inarticulate, and it occurs to me now that I know many who write poetry this way or have written it at one time, not to be published, not even to show to others, except maybe a trusted friend, but to give words to things in their hearts that are without words, to give words in verse, it may be, or in prose—it may be simply in a diary. A discovery occurs when I give words to thoughts of the heart, a decision too, at least to acknowledge them if not to follow them.

If I acknowledge the thoughts of my heart to others, if I follow them so far as to share them with others, I am speaking in the second voice of poetry, the voice addressing an audience, and my desire has become a desire to be known, to be understood. "The difficult resolution" for me is sometimes simply to give words to the thoughts of my heart in order to understand them myself, sometimes to go on and share them and be understood by others. There is a desire I can feel, and yet also a fear, of being known, of being understood. Reading, according to Proust, is essentially "a communication in the midst of solitude"[17] where I come to understand the thoughts of other hearts without communicating my own in return. Writing is that too, from the other side, where I communicate thoughts of my own heart to others without them communicating theirs to me in return. Thus reading, and writing too, as Proust understands it, is a kind of one-way

conversation. The solitude of it, though, the solitude in the
midst of communication, can make me long for something
more, for a communion of thoughts and of hearts.

Now my desire is taking the shape of a desire to know and
be known, to hold communion with others, like my desire
"to hold communion with other living things." Only now,
after my contact with "thoughts of the heart," it is a desire
to know and love, to be known and loved, to enter fully
into human intercourse. My writing now becomes like my
reading, a passing over into the thoughts and the hearts of
others, like speaking in the third voice of poetry, the voice assuming the person of a character in a play, as "all the world's
a stage, and all the men and women merely players." But I
come again on Jonson's question, "Where shall we find the
spectators of their plays?" and Shakespeare's answer, "We're
all both actors and spectators too." I have certainly been a
spectator, and now I want to be a player, but the spectator
being included in the play is like the observer being included
in the interactions of quantum physics. It leads to "relations
of uncertainty."[18]

If the spectator and the player in me cannot be separated, I mean, if the desire to know cannot be separated
from the desire to be known, then there is an uncertainty
in the knowing. I find in myself a longing not just for a
pure spectator's certainty, to know that I know, but for a
spectator/player's certainty, to know that I am understood,
and that comes up against the solitude I experience in the
midst of communication. "There is no one here who wholly
understands me," Kafka writes in his diary. "To have one
person with this understanding, a woman for example, that
would be to have a foothold on every side, it would mean to
have God."[19] I have often meditated on these lonely words—
I came across them first in Max Brod's life of Kafka. I think
now the situation may have been one of uncertainty. It is not
that there was no one he could turn to, but there was no one
he could turn to and know he was understood, as one might
turn to God. As I read and write, as I pass over to others and
come back again to myself, I can feel the solitude he speaks

of, and yet I can also see the "fruitful miracle," as Proust calls it, "of a communication in the midst of solitude."

It seems if I can consent to solitude in the midst of communication, if I can consent to communication in the midst of solitude, I can find "this understanding" that Kafka speaks of, I can "have a foothold on every side," I can "have God." "It seems that this happiness did come his way at the end of his life," Brod goes on to say of Kafka, "and that the outcome of his fate was more positive and more full of life than its whole previous development."[20] Kafka did find the woman he spoke of, "a woman for example," in Dora Dymant who became his life's companion in his last years. Still, it is in the relationship with the person, it seems to me, and not just in the particular person that the solution resides. There is a solitude in the midst of every communication, it seems, in every conversation, however two-way, in every form of human intercourse. If I can embrace solitude and at the same time embrace communication, I can be at heartsease in knowing and being known, in loving and being loved.

There is a kind of reading, *lectio divina* as it is called in the monasteries, where the "fruitful miracle of a communication in the midst of solitude" seems to take on these dimensions of a sense of being understood, of having support on every side, of having God. As I understand it, *lectio divina*, "divine reading,"[21] is a kind of meditative and prayerful reading, especially of scripture, that lets the words speak to the heart, whenever they will. Say I am reading the Psalms, and I come upon this verse,

> The counsel of the Lord stands forever,
> the thoughts of his heart to all generations.[22]

Say it speaks to the emotion or situation in which I find myself, and to the style or will I bring to the situation. The thoughts of my heart, the thoughts of other hearts, it seems to say, are not like "the thoughts of his heart." And at a time when I feel overwhelmed by the thoughts of my heart and by the thoughts of other hearts, this gives me a courage that is freedom and a freedom that is happiness. And I respond in prayer, "Lord, reveal your heart to me, reveal to me the thoughts of your heart. Give me courage; give me freedom; give me the happiness only you can give."

My embracing of solitude, my embracing of communication, enables me to hear and to understand not only the voices of poetry therefore but also the voice of prayer. When we bring solitude and communication together, we are "receiving the communication of another thought, while we remain alone," Proust says, ". . . while continuing to be inspired, to maintain the mind's full, fruitful work on itself."[23] The mind's work on itself is recollection, I think he means, bringing time to mind. As I bring my own lifetime to mind, I come into touch in solitude with the thoughts of my own heart. Meanwhile in communication, in passing over to others, I come into touch with the thoughts of other hearts. As my mind works on itself, the thoughts of other hearts meet those of my own heart, and as our past becomes present to me, I enter into a timeless presence where time past and time present are one, where the thoughts of our heart can meet the eternal thoughts of God.

Reading the Gospels, particularly the Gospel of Luke, where there are passages like canticles, and trying to recapture the experience of *lectio divina*, Proust says, "I have heard the silence of the worshipper who has just stopped reading aloud in order to sing the succeeding verses like a psalm." What Proust finds here is the Past, "the perfume of a rose . . . which had not evaporated for seventeen centuries."[24] If I read with faith, though, sharing in the hope, in the willingness as well as in "the silence of the worshipper," I find more than "the Past familiarly risen in the midst of the present." I find an eternal presence. It is true, I do not know the thoughts of God. I know only that I do not know, only that "my thoughts are not your thoughts,"[25] as Isaiah says, speaking for God. I can nevertheless open my mind and heart to the thoughts of God's heart, opening them almost like opening my eyes after squinting, allowing the light that comes to illumine the thoughts of my own heart and the thoughts of other hearts that I keep in my heart. I can allow my mind to be illumined, that is, and my heart to be kindled.

I can open my mind and heart to what is revealed according to the Gospel of John, "And the Word became flesh and dwelt among us," simply by letting the words of the Gospel, "the words of eternal life,"[26] speak to my heart. It is as if Christ were a child in God's lap, "in the bosom of the Father," and were revealing the thoughts of God's heart to me, as to a beloved disciple, "lying close to the breast of Jesus."[27] Still, I do not come simply by reading to know the thoughts of God's heart. Reading John, "we would like to have him give us answers, while all he can do is give us desires," as Proust said of other reading. "And these desires he can arouse in us only by making us contemplate the supreme beauty which the last effort of his art has permitted him to reach." What I find, reading John, is my heart kindled, my mind illumined by a sense of presence.

It is through the sense of presence that I come to know whatever I know of the thoughts of God's heart. "The guiding counsel of God seems to me to be simply the divine Presence," Martin Buber says, "communicating itself direct to the pure in heart."[28] When I am at a crossroads, Buber is saying, and I ask God to show me the way, the response I seem to get from God in prayer is simply "I am with you." I feel like replying to God, "But actually what I wanted to know was which way to go." Yet "I am with you," the simple sense of the presence of God, does help, does support me, although it does not take away the agony of decision. It gives me the courage, the freedom to make a choice. So it is one thing simply to choose and another to choose in the presence. So too, when I am reading the Gospel of John, I come upon the "I am" sayings of Jesus, very like the "I am with you" in response to my prayers for light. Instead of articulating the thoughts of God's heart, "I am" seems simply to express the sense of God's presence. And yet the sense of presence does illuminate the thoughts of my own heart.

Now it is just the sense of presence, or rather "the metaphysics of presence," that deconstruction sets out to deconstrue. To relate words only to words, as is done in deconstruction, and not to real presences is "to risk meaning nothing," as Jacques Derrida himself acknowledges, and "to risk meaning nothing is to start to play."[29] The words of the Gospel of John are about words, but they are about words that become flesh, about words of eternal life. There is the risk of meaning nothing, there is the beginning of play, and yet there is the presence of "I am." Let us see now what may happen if we relate words not just to words but to music.

The Way of Music

To put words to music is also "to risk meaning nothing" and "to start to play," for without words music can seem to point to nothing beyond itself. "He is so simple that he is meaningless. His music *disappears*, like the air we breathe on a transparent day," Turner says of Mozart. "Such a day does not provoke or in the faintest degree suggest one mood rather than another. It is infinitely protean. It means just what you mean." Or so it seems at first. "*Then* suddenly there will pass through you a tremor of terror. A moment comes when that tranquillity, that perfection will take on a ghastly ambiguity," he says. "That music still suggests nothing, nothing at all, it is just infinitely ambiguous."[30] He goes on then to speak of the "demoniacal clang" of Mozart. There is something then after all in a music that seems otherwise to be pure play, pure transparency, meaning nothing beyond itself. Something does show through the transparency, something does come about in the play. What is it? A presence maybe, or an absence where the presence ought to be, an absence that can seem a "demoniacal clang." Or is it indeed a presence, an elusive presence that can seem an absence?

There is such a thing as "the practice of the presence of God," a practice of attention, as "attention is the natural prayer of the soul,"[31] a devotion that consists not so much in applying more energy to thinking as in directing your thinking to a point of origin. It may be essential "to risk

meaning nothing," as Mozart did, and "to start to play," in
order to evoke the presence of God. In Gregorian chant,
where the words are considered sacred, there is a great freedom in the music, a free rhythm that allows the music to
follow the rhythm of the words, but also a kind of freedom
of melody that allows the words to follow the rise and fall
of the music, carrying the syllables of the words over as
many notes as desired, stretching the vowels of *alleluia*, for
instance, over many intervals. So chant too comes "to risk
meaning nothing" and "to start to play." There is a presence,
nevertheless, accessible in the words and in the music.

If music can be a practice of the presence of God, a practice of attention, "the natural prayer of the soul," it can be so
not just for the listener, as listening is paying attention, but
also for the performer, the listening performer, and also for
the composer, "the listening composer." It is true, in listening to music you may be doing anything but practicing the
presence of God. Consider this passage from E. M. Forster's
novel, *Howards End*:

> It will be generally admitted that Beethoven's Fifth Sym-
> phony is the most sublime noise that has ever penetrated into
> the ear of man. All sorts and conditions are satisfied by it.
> Whether you are like Mrs. Munt, and tap surreptitiously when
> the tunes come—of course, not so as to disturb the others—;
> or like Helen, who can see heroes and shipwrecks in the
> music's flood; or like Margaret, who can only see the music;
> or like Tibby, who is profoundly versed in counterpoint, and
> holds the full score open on his knee . . .

"in any case," Forster concludes, "the passion of your life
becomes more vivid."[32] To pass from these ways of listening
to a listening in which "attention is the natural prayer of
the soul" is to pass from time to eternity. It is to realize that
time, as Plato said, is "a changing image of eternity," that
the rhythm is of time, that the music's flood is changing
image, that the music is of eternity, that the counterpoint
is its temporal structure. It is to let a new fire kindle, a new
light illumine "the passion of your life."

To listen this way is to listen with an ancient ear. It is to listen like Augustine who in his dialogue *On Music* wanted to pass from music in time to eternal music. "How I wept during your hymns and songs!" he exclaims to God in his *Confessions.* "The sounds flowed into my ears and the truth was distilled into my heart."[33] It is true, further on he is worried about taking too much pleasure in music, but he concludes with Plato that the soul and music are akin. "All the diverse emotions of our spirit have their various modes in voice and chant appropriate in each case," he says, "and are stirred by a mysterious inner kinship." Let us see what it would be for composing, for performing, for listening, to be aware of this kinship, to hear eternal music in the song of earth.

It is Forster's remark, "in any case, the passion of your life becomes more vivid," that points the way. It suggests that we bring something to music, we bring the passion of our life, whatever it may be, and music, listening to music, makes that passion more vivid. Say the passion of my life is knowledge, or knowledge of some kind. Say it is love, or love of some kind, human love, or maybe the love of God. Whatever it is, it becomes more vivid when I am moved by listening to music. Since I am bringing the passion of my life to the music, I am not really discovering it there, as if the music were the expression of that knowledge or that love. All the music does is make the passion more vivid. It kindles my passion and illumines my life. "It means just what you mean," as Turner says of Mozart's music, and that seems true also of Beethoven's music, according to Forster's description, but "then suddenly" the music will become "infinitely ambiguous," as if there were something there, other than "the passion of your life," something that can pierce you to the heart. It is something eternal, I want to say, and it resonates with the eternal in us.

Remembering "musical moments," I remember times, usually after playing the piano at some length by myself, when I seemed carried into another world. It could be said, according to the bicameral theory of the brain, that I was being carried from the verbal into the nonverbal side of the brain. As I experienced it, though, and still do, it is an experience of being carried from one world into another. "Do you mean this world or is there another?" Violane is asked. "There are two," she answers, "but I say there is only one and that is enough."[34] There is one world, it seems to me too, and it is not just the world of words, "the universe of discourse," but also the world of music. It is the greater world of words and music. There is an exhilaration you feel when you enter this greater world, and there is a feeling, as in storytelling, that time does not matter.

"To escape from the sense of time, to live in the eternity of what he was accustomed to call 'the divine essence of things'—that was his only desire."[35] And that is what "the passion of your life" becomes as it "becomes more vivid," a passion to live in the eternity, in the divine essence of the things you love. I may love someone, I may love something, but as the passion of my life becomes more vivid it becomes a desire to live in the timeless essence of my love, to be always with that someone, that something that I love. It is not that music dissolves time into eternity. Rather time in music becomes indeed "a changing image of eternity." Time is the movement of music, the tempo, the rhythm, the flow of melody. Eternity is the repose in movement, the rest in restlessness. No doubt, to listen with an ancient ear is to be able to hear not only the major and minor modes of classical music but also the many ancient modes, Dorian, Phrygian, Lydian and the rest, as well as the pentatonic modes of folk music and so too the whole-tone and twelve-tone modes of later music. Still, it is not the discernment of modes or of intervals such as tritones so much as pure attention, being absorbed in the flowing movement of musical time, that brings you to a sense of timeless presence.

It is said of jazz that music becomes "a state of being" rather than "symbolic form"[36] with a beginning, a middle, and an ending. There is something of this in all music as it becomes a practice of attention, a practice of presence. What I mean here by being absorbed, though, is a conscious

attention, not a relative loss of consciousness. I mean a conscious feeling of the kinship of the music and the soul. I think
of T. S. Eliot listening to Beethoven's last string quartets and
writing his own last poems, *Four Quartets.* There is no one-to-
one correspondence between the six string quartets and the
four poems. It is more a matter of passing from a "symbolic
form," that of the string quartets, through music as "a state
of being," to another "symbolic form," that of the poems.
In composing, on the other hand, there is a passing the
other way, through music as "a state of being" to music as
"symbolic form."

Attention, like love, is essentially a direction, but it can become "a state of being." According to Paul Celan it is "a kind
of concentration mindful of all our dates."[37] Timeless presence comes with bringing time to mind, that is, with being
"mindful of all our dates." The past and the future become
present to us, and all is at once in a presence where time
does not lapse. My concentration becomes musical when I
begin to improvise. Here too jazz, as a kind of continuous
improvization, is a model. When I am improvising, I am
listening and performing and composing. I can do it with
my voice, just humming, or with a musical instrument, playing, or simply with my imagination, hearing in the silence.
But there is a further step in composing and that is to pass
from improvising to "symbolic form." Consider the following
passage from a letter of Mozart:

> When I feel well and in a good humor, or when I am taking
> a drive or walking after a good meal, or in the night when I
> cannot sleep, thoughts crowd into my mind as easily as you
> could wish. Whence and how do they come? I do not know
> and I have nothing to do with it. Those which please me, I
> keep in my head and hum them; at least others have told me
> that I do so. Once I have my theme, another melody comes,
> linking itself to the first one, in accordance with the needs
> of the composition as a whole: the counterpoint, the part
> of each instrument, and all these melodic fragments at last
> produce the entire work. Then my soul is on fire with in-
> spiration, if however nothing occurs to distract my attention.

The work grows; I keep expanding it, conceiving it more and more clearly until I have the entire composition finished in my head though it may be long. Then my mind seizes it as a glance of my eye a beautiful picture or a handsome youth. It does not come to me successively, with its various parts worked out in detail, as they will be later on, but it is in its entirety that my imagination lets me hear it.[38]

A similar process occurs in spontaneous prayer, and in spontaneous song. There is an improvising of words and of music, there is "a state of being," but without the structural finish of "symbolic form." Instead of being able to perceive the whole, as Mozart did ("it is in its entirety that my imagination lets me hear it"), you are led along step by step, one step at a time. Still, the earlier part of what Mozart said holds true. "When I feel well. . .when I cannot sleep, thoughts crowd into my mind as easily as you could wish. Whence and how do they come? I do not know and I have nothing to do with it." When you begin to pray or to sing, you begin to choose among those thoughts, some of them or maybe all of them. "Those which please me, I keep in my head and hum them; at least others have told me that I do so." And as you go on, you may come to feel "my soul is on fire with inspiration," but then you have to add, "if however nothing occurs to distract my attention."

These "thoughts" Mozart speaks of that "crowd into my mind as easily as you could wish" are like the "thoughts" Shakespeare speaks of that "people this little world." They are "thoughts of the heart," *cogitationes cordis,* and they people this little world of words or that other world of music or the greater world of words and music. I think of the scene Yeats describes in *A Vision,* when he was on the coast of Normandy, and saw, as he walked along the shore, a young woman singing out toward the sea, singing to words and music of her own, singing of all the peoples who had lived and died on those shores, all the civilizations that had come and gone, and ending each stanza with the refrain, "O Lord, let something remain!"[39] This is what I mean by spontaneous prayer and song. The thoughts of her heart were becoming words and music. In her concentration she was "mindful of all our dates," things she kept and pondered in her heart, peoples and civilizations, but some things came from within her, and her heart's desire was in that refrain, "O Lord, let something remain!" She was an icon for Yeats of our longing for eternal life, and she is an icon for me of the words and the music of the heart.

Everyone has a song, I believe, just as everyone has a story, and everyone has a heart's desire. To actually sing the song is another thing, to tell the story, to follow the heart's desire. I was once paging through a collection of unwritten songs from around the world when I came upon this one, an African love song consisting of the single sentence, "I walk alone."[40] This is what I mean by the song everyone has, a simple expression of heart's desire like "I walk alone" or "O Lord, let something remain!" A person's song is a theme that is capable of endless variations, a song that can become many songs. If in listening to music "the passion of your life becomes more vivid," it is just this, "the passion of your life," that is expressed in your own song. If I ask myself "What is your song?" I am asking myself "What is the passion of your life?"

If I ask myself these questions, I think of a melody that came to me forty years ago and a name that I learned ten years ago when I was in Istanbul, the name Ayasofya.[41] It is the Turkish name for Hagia Sophia, a church for a thousand years, a mosque for five hundred years, and now an empty monument. The name means "Holy Wisdom," though, and I use it as if it were the personal name of the figure of Wisdom that is spoken of in the book of Proverbs, the figure Vladimir Solovyov speaks of meeting in his poem "Three Meetings." A young Turkish woman once said to me, "You are in love with Ayasofya!" Here is the melody of the song:

The melody is repeated through a series of harmonic changes like those of Bach's Prelude in C. There is only one word, Ayasofya, repeated over and over, like an *alleluia* in Gregorian chant. It suggests the passion of a life in pursuit of wisdom.

As I personify the figure of Wisdom and invoke her in my song as Ayasofya, I think of Dante and the figure of Beatrice and his song in *terza rima*. I think again of Kafka saying "There is no one here who wholly understands me. To have one person with this understanding, a woman for example, that would be to have a foothold on every side, it would mean to have God." If a person's song is a theme with many variations, it can be hard to tell which are variations and which is the theme itself. It can be hard to tell which expression of heart's desire comes nearest to what Lacan calls "the real of desire." Is it the more concrete expression, "a woman for example," or is it the more spiritual expression, like the figure of Wisdom, or is it a transformation of the one into the other, as the theme goes through the variations, like the figure of Beatrice? Music itself can be a way of finding out, as "the passion of your life becomes more vivid."

If I follow the path of "the worshipper" that Proust describes "who has just stopped reading aloud in order to sing the succeeding verses like a psalm," I find that singing carries my heart from the concrete to the spiritual and back again. Consider the words Igor Stravinsky chooses to set to music in his *Symphony of Psalms*.[42] The first movement sets the ending of one psalm, "Hear my prayer, O Lord. . . ." The second movement sets the beginning of the next psalm, "Waiting, I waited on the Lord. . . ." And the third movement sets the last of all the psalms, "Alleluia! Praise the Lord!..." There is a progression here from praying to praising. The climax is the high singing of *alleluia* alternating with the low singing of *laudate*, as if singing were to reach the heights of the spiritual and yet to encompass the depths of the concrete in our life. Both the Hebrew word *alleluia* and the Latin word *laudate* mean the same thing, "Praise!" What happens in music is somehow a fulfillment of the command to love "with all your heart, and with all your soul, and with all your might," where love ranges from the heights to the depths of your being.

I had thought to say there is an ascent in music, like that of Platonic love, from passion for the concrete individual to ecstasy in contemplation of the spiritual ideal, and what I find instead is a coming to wholeness of spirit, like David who "danced before the Lord with all his might."[43] The *alleluia* in the heights is matched by the *laudate* in the depths. There is at once an ascent into the heights and a descent into the depths, a kind of entering into sympathy with all humanity, with all that is human, a kind of humility. There is the secret! "Humility provides every one, even the lonely and despairing, with the firmest relation to one's fellow human beings," Kafka says, "a relation, too, that is instantaneous, though only if the humility is complete and permanent. It can do this," he adds, "because it is the true language of prayer, at once worship and firmest union."[44] That is what music is, I believe, "the true language of prayer, at once worship and firmest union."

Bach and Beethoven "walked with God," it has been said. "Mozart did not. Mozart danced with the masked daughters of Vienna and wasted his spirit. . . ."[45] Yet the truth may be that Mozart danced also with God. There is that in his music that is "the true language of prayer, at once worship and firmest union." No doubt, Mozart is a master of music as "symbolic form," but there is also in his music "a state of being." There is in his music an ascent from passion to ecstasy in contemplation, an ascent that does not leave the individual behind, but encompasses the whole human range in a balance of opposites that is felt as a kind of serenity. It is that serenity that is most felt in his music as "a state of being," not passion, not ecstasy. It is that serenity then that is ambiguous, that can seem to have a "demoniacal clang," that can seem to lack passion, to lack ecstasy, to lack humanity and therefore to be inhuman. There is a clue here for us. When I am at one with the passion of my life, however vivid, when I am at one with my heart's desire, saying "Thanks!" and "Yes!" I am not passionate, I am not ecstatic, I am serene, I am at peace.

There is "religion as anxiety," it has been said, and there is "religion as tranquillity."[46] The movement of "the true language of prayer," though, is from anxiety to tranquillity, from anxiety really to serenity and peace. "To escape from the sense of time, to live in the eternity of what he was accustomed to call 'the divine essence of things'—that was his only desire." And that is the desire that is fulfilled in passing from anxiety to peace. Here is the answer to our question, "Do the voices that are heard in poetry tell us of the essence of things?" When music and poetry "disappears," like the music of Mozart, "like the air we breathe on a transparent day," when we pass from anxiety to serenity, then we live in the eternity of "the divine essence of things." Thus *the essence of things is not opaque, it is transparent, it is translucent to the presence of God in the words and the music of the heart.*

Yet what of the "demoniacal clang"? It is the shadow cast by the light of translucence and transparency. It is the echo of "religion as anxiety." It is "the octupus or angel with which the poet struggles"[47] according to T. S. Eliot. The octupus becomes an angel as I pass from "religion as anxiety" to "religion as tranquillity" in words and music, but the "demoniacal clang" is there to remind me of the uncertainty I am coming from and to which I am always returning. As I sing to Holy Wisdom, for example, the "demoniacal clang" is there to remind me there is "no fool like an old fool," to remind me of the uncertainty that makes me vulnerable to foolishness. It is true, I want to eliminate the disturbance it brings to my peace of mind. Still, I do not want to separate the figure of Wisdom from her human incarnations in my life, or to stop listening to human words in order to hear divine words. For here too it holds true, "And the Word became flesh and dwelt among us," and it is through human words that God speaks to my heart. I am left therefore with an uncertainty that is at times opaque, at times translucent, at times transparent.

When it is transparent I live in the eternity of "the divine essence of things"; when it is translucent I live in a bright time where eternity shines through; when it is opaque I live in a dark time, troubled by regret and fear, and it is then I have to live in uncertainty without despairing, in "religion as anxiety." Yet there in a dark time I discover "dread as a saving experience by means of faith,"[48] as Kierkegaard describes it; I let dread become prayer, let it become a cry to God, as in the first movement of Stravinsky's *Symphony of Psalms,* and I come to a sense of being heard, as in the second movement, and my prayer ends in praise, as in the third movement, in the high *alleluia* and the deep *laudate.* I am able thus to pass through the darkness of time to the brightness of eternity in time.

Time's mystery is hidden when time is dark with regret and fear. When I say "mystery," I mean "that which shows itself and at the same time withdraws."[49] The mystery that shows itself and hides itself in time is eternity, a timeless presence. When I am caught up in regret and fear, eternity is in eclipse and I am aware only of the past I regret and the future I fear. When I let the words and the music of the heart carry me beyond regret and fear, on the other hand, I become aware of the timeless presence shining through time. There is method in this; there is method in the words and the music of the heart. Looking for "a method for breathing an inspiration into a people," Simone Weil has it "there is a method to be followed in spiritual matters and in everything connected with the soul's welfare."[50] I see such a method, for instance, in Stravinsky's setting of the psalms, starting with the cry of the heart, and going on to the sense of being heard, and ending in the joy of heart's content. Let us try out these three movements of contemplation as a method, as a way to heart's desire.

Three Movements
of Contemplation

"I know I am traveling all the time"
— Artur Lundkvist

"Who knows where memory begins?" Who knows, that is, where real presence leaves off and presence only in memory begins. It is a question you might ask yourself when you have lost someone you love. "Who can say where the vibrant voice becomes an echo, the face once so vividly intaglioed on the retina a fading copy in the mind?"[1] Or can presence in memory be real? If it can be real, then love is never really lost. It is true, "memory is not what the heart desires," as Tolkien says, unless "memory is more like to the waking world than to a dream."[2] And memory is that in contemplation, for contemplation is living and moving and having your being in eternal presence.

Contemplation is remembering God. There are three movements of contemplation, according to Aquinas, the circular, the straight, and the oblique.[3] The circular is around God (with "simple intuition"), the straight is from the world to God (from "sensible things to intelligible things"), and the oblique is with God in the world (following "divine illuminations"). "Do you still remember God?" the stranger is asked in Rilke's *Stories of God*. In the stranger's eyes you can see long, shaded avenues leading back to what seems a point of light. "Yes," he answers, "I still remember God."[4] The circular movement of contemplation is to gaze upon the point of light, as if you were a moth circling around it.

53

The straight movement is to pass along those long shaded avenues to the point of light, "the exit on the far side into a perhaps much brighter day." The oblique movement is to come back along those avenues with the light at your back, lighting up the way ahead for you. In the circular movement you almost forget all loss in time. In the straight movement you let your loss in time carry you into eternal presence. In the oblique movement you let eternal light lead you on into time once more.

Circular, straight, oblique, this is a sequence for the mind, going from simplicity to complexity. But is it also a sequence for the heart? As "our heart is restless until it rests in you,"[5] we cannot begin with the heart in repose. We must begin with the movement of restlessness, the heart going from one thing to another, finding no rest and crying out to God. Yet that is just what the circular movement is, going from one thing to another, finding no rest, circling like a moth around a point of light. The straight movement to the point of light begins when the heart cries out to God, when heart speaks to heart and comes to a sense of being heard. The oblique movement begins then when the light becomes the "kindly light" as in Newman's prayer "Lead, kindly light," the light showing the way, leading us on the road of the heart's desire.

"I know I am traveling all the time,"[6] Artur Lundkvist writes of his experience of his life being taken out of his hands. "The hallucinatory memoir of a poet in a coma," he calls it. He is in a hospital bed, but he is traveling all the time, he says, "in dream and imagination." Let us see what it would be to travel all the time in contemplation, where "memory is more like to the waking world than to a dream." Let us see what it would be to go on a journey of the heart from restlessness to repose in light.

The Restless Heart

"I know I am traveling all the time," Lundkvist begins, and he ends, "you journey towards the end as empty-handed as in the beginning, old age, gravestone leaning over you, its shadow ever growing."[7] Is there nothing that points beyond death, I wonder, that points, as Henri Nouwen says of a similar experience, "beyond the mirror"?[8] Death is a mirror in our anticipation, a mirror in which we see ourselves and our lives. It is "a mirror of scorn and pity"[9] like the mirror storytelling holds up to the human, according to Tolkien, for we can see ourselves and our lives with scorn and pity in the light of our death. But death, like storytelling, seems to have another face turned towards nature, that of "magic," as it is the means by which one thing is transformed into another. And it has still another face, like storytelling too, turned towards the divine, that of "mystery." *What does the heart's desire look like in the mirror of death, in the magic of transfiguration, and in the mystery of eternal life?*

In the mirror we see the restless movement of the heart, going from one person to another, from one enthusiasm to another, a kind of perpetual motion that seems to cease only with death. Here the heart of thought and feeling is not unlike the heart beating in the body. Only there is always a "beyond the mirror" for thought and for feeling. As I remember, as I retrace the restless movement of my own heart, I think of something a friend once said after reading a number of tales of love. "If love is intimate, it cannot be lasting," he concluded. "If love is lasting, it cannot be intimate." That is what you would expect to see in "a mirror of scorn and pity." Yet is it true? Is intimate love never lasting? Is lasting love never intimate? As I remember the loves of my own life, I can feel the scorn and the pity of the mirror.

"Beyond the mirror," though, I can look for more. When Heinrich Böll's clown looks in the mirror, he makes faces at himself, but when he sees himself in Marie's eyes, he sees love rather than scorn and pity.[10] It is already something, given the restlessness of the heart, that love can be lasting. It is possible to interpret this restless movement, going from one thing to another, as the *neti neti* of the Upanishads, the "not this, not that" of the negative way to God. That is how Aquinas begins his Summas, with the *via negativa,* and that is probably what he has in mind when he speaks of "the circular movement of contemplation."[11] If I am not mistaken, it is a way of interpreting the restlessness of desire. As I go from one person to another, from one enthusiasm to another, I realize what I want is "not this, not that" but God alone. To interpret my restlessness in this way, I mean, is to realize God is my heart's desire, and God is what I am seeking and not finding in "this" and "that." It is this interpretation, this realization, that turns the restless movement into the circular movement of contemplation.

Is interpretation enough? Does realization change the heart or does it change only the mind? Before I come to this interpretation, this realization, I am indeed like a moth, mindless in my fascination, circling around the light. To interpret my restlessness then in this way, to realize I am moving in circles, around a center, to realize it is God I desire, is to come to know my heart. Let us see how far knowing the heart can change the heart.

"At that precise moment," Marcel Marceau says at the end of a story, "Pimporello had already become a little moving point, lost in timeless infinity." It is a moment of interpretation, a moment of realization, of coming to know the heart. It seems to connect with the way Marceau begins, "Mime is the art of telling stories in silence, in which movement becomes a way of expressing thought."[12] It is as though the movements of my life express the movements of my heart and thereby express thought, although it may be a thought that I have yet consciously to think. When I do think the thought, when I come to know my heart, I become "a little moving point, lost in timeless infinity." The movements of my life have been "telling stories in silence." Coming to know my heart is like breaking the silence and telling the story in words, as Marceau, the master of mime, is doing in this story of Pimporello, the street mime. It is as though I too have been a mime, telling my story in silence, and now, coming to know my heart, I have begun to speak.

To be "a little moving point, lost in timeless infinity" is to be at peace with myself and yet to be on a great journey. I take being "lost in timeless infinity" not as having lost my way but as being encompassed, being surrounded. "I know I am traveling all the time," I can still say, but to think of myself as "a little moving point, lost in timeless infinity" is to be aware of something more. It is to be aware not only of time and of restlessness but of timeless infinity and of rest. "Our heart is restless," moving from one image to another, "until it rests in you," moving from image to insight. Yet coming to insight doesn't seem to stop the movement from image to image. It only means becoming conscious of the timeless infinity in which I am moving. It is the sense of being encompassed, of being "lost in timeless infinity" that gives me rest.

Now I have changed the metaphor from circling around a light to being a moving point in an expanse of light. I have passed really from the circular to the straight and oblique movements of contemplation. Not so quick! What we need to know here is how to get from restlessness to rest, from images to insight. The restless movement of the heart is from image to image, not only when you are in a hospital bed like Artur Lundkvist and are traveling "in dream and imagination" but also when you are up and about but moving from one enthusiasm to another, from one person to another. Each situation, each person is overlayed with imagination, as in the story of Don Quixote, and your sense of yourself too is overlayed with imagination, like Don Quixote coming back from his first sally and saying "I know who I am,"[13] or like the street mime in Marcel Marceau's story, meeting the little orphan Nina and telling her he has been a great circus clown and then even getting a part in a circus, making his dream come true. There comes a moment in the story when everything comes untrue again, when Don Quixote comes back from his second sally and says "I know that I am enchanted," or when Marceau's street mime is alone again, wondering if there really was a little orphan girl who so resembled his lost daughter, wondering if there really was a circus.

It is a moment of doubt, of disillusion, when you realize images are only images. It can become a moment of insight, though, as you pass from "telling stories in silence" to breaking the silence with "the words and the music." Marcel Marceau speaks of "my two masters" and says, "The first taught me speech; the second, silence."[14] So silence is something that can be taught, something that requires mastery, and "telling stories in silence" is an art, that of mime.

Silence as an art, as a mastery, is a way "to hold life up to death," as Marceau says, "light up to shadow, and dreams up to reality."[15] Silence can have a role like that also in "the words and the music." If indeed "we can know more than we can tell,"[16] as Michael Polanyi says, there is always a "tacit dimension" in words, the unsaid present in the said, and in music, the unsung present in the sung. Say there is a repeating pattern in my relations with others, like the refrain of a song repeated after each stanza. Say my relations with others are intimate but not lasting—then the tacit dimension of my life is the lasting. Say my relations are lasting but not intimate—then the tacit dimension is the intimate. To hold life up to death, light up to shadow, and dreams up to reality in my life thus is to hold the missing or tacit dimension of the lasting up to the intimate, of the intimate up to the lasting. If I actually put my repeating pattern of relation into words and music, I come up with love songs haunted by the lasting, like Donne's early poetry, or with mystical songs, like his later poetry, haunted by the intimate.

It is clear that both the lasting and the intimate belong to my life. I keep moving restlessly from image to image because I have taken a road on which love is lasting but not intimate, or intimate but not lasting, and I am haunted always by the road I have not taken. The restless movement comes to rest, time comes to a standstill, only when I remember, when I bring time to mind. It is as if every one of the persons of my life were saying one and the same thing, "Remember me." I think of Augustine, how his heart was restless and did not find rest simply in his conversion, his turning to God, but continued on afterwards, it seems, until he found healing and wholeness in his *Confessions,* telling and yet knowing more than he could tell, finding peace in knowing and being known.

"To hold life up to death, light up to shadow, and dreams up to reality" is to hold life and light and love up to the mirror of death. It is to remember life in the face of death, to remember light in the face of shadow, to remember dreams in the face of reality. It is, in remembering all else, to remember God. "Take and read," the command Augustine heard in his moment of conversion, leads directly to that other command, "Remember me." Reading and remembering are linked, especially if reading is understood with Proust as "a communication in solitude." For remembering is that too, and it can be a communication of life and light and love in solitude, when the will is turned to God, when remembering the persons of my life, remembering the enthusiasms, is re-membering God. I hold life up to death when in the prospect of death I remember all I have loved, when I remember, as is said in the Gospel of John, "those whom thou has given me."[17] I hold light up to shadow when I affirm them in spite of the shadow that may have fallen on our relationship. And I hold dreams up to reality when I link memory with hope.

"This last should be easiest," Marcel Marceau says of his street mime, "since his own dreams had always been real and his reality had always been filled with dreams."[18] Linking memory with hope, I ask myself "What may I hope?" My dreams too have always been real, I can see as I remember, and my reality has always been filled with dreams. So when I ask myself what I may hope, I have to discern between dreams and reality and yet to hold dreams up to reality, to hold possibility, that is, up to reality. False hopes appear false as I discern between dreams and reality, but I discover a way of possibility as I hold my dreams up to reality, a way on which false hopes turn to good hope as mimetic desires turn to heart's desire. "I am too old, and the seas are too long," Francis Bacon said, "for me to double the Cape of Good Hope."[19] Still, I have to round that cape in my life, however old I am, however long the seas, I have to come to good hope if my false hopes are not to turn to despair.

I come to good hope by acknowledging the eternal in me. If I acknowledge only the time of my life, there comes a point when "I am too old, and the seas are too long, for me to double the Cape of Good Hope." Consider Heidegger's question, "Am I my time?"[20] If I say "Yes," my hope is within the horizon of my time and ends with my death. If I say "No," I am making a distinction between my time and myself, between the life and the person living the life. There is hope in that distinction. It is true, if I am asked "Who are you?" there are two ways of answering, one is to tell my name, the other is to tell my story. The one points to the person, the other to the life the person lives. But if I tell my story, I become aware of the untold, how "we can know more than we can tell," and that "more" contains a hint of hope. I think of the wise woman George MacDonald describes in one of his stories who "knew something too good to be told."[21] If in fact "we can know more than we can tell," we can know something too good to be told, something we can know without knowing that we know it, something about who we are.

It is the eternal in us, from which "hope springs eternal." It is the source of the life we hold up to death, of the light we hold up to shadow, of the dreams we hold up to reality. The circular movement of contemplation circles around the eternal in us, around God in us. When Polanyi says "we can know more than we can tell," he has in mind "the particulars" we know of "a comprehensive entity."[22] When I tell the story of my life, the comprehensive entity is myself and the particulars are in Shakespeare's words "the particulars of my life." It is the comprehensive entity, though, myself, the eternal in me, God in me, that I am seeking to know in telling my story. Augustine prays "that I may know me, that I may know thee,"[23] and Tolstoy, when he is trying to tell Gorky what he means by saying "God is my desire," says "I must have wanted to say 'God is my desire to know Him'. . . No, not that" and then laughs and says no more.[24]

To know me, to know thee, is my heart's desire. It is intimacy with the eternal in us, and is thus the answer to the dilemma, "If love is intimate, it cannot be lasting; if love is lasting, it cannot be intimate." All I have, though, is the desire. All I have is the prayer, "that I may know me, that I may know thee." As my desire becomes a prayer, nevertheless, and I consciously ask God for this intimacy with the eternal in us, I am taking a long step into knowledge of myself and knowledge of God. My restless desire, moving from one person to another, from one enthusiasm to another, is becoming through prayer a conscious desire to know me, to know thee, a conscious "I and thou" with God. Prayer, I begin to see, is conscious desire and is the means by which desire becomes conscious, the means by which mimetic desire turns to heart's desire and false hopes turn to good hope. Prayer, I say, not yet the answer to prayer but prayer itself. By praying to know me, to know thee, I become conscious of desiring to know me, to know thee, I become conscious that "God is my desire" and has been my desire all along.

Prayer is the expression of the heart's desire, and it is the means by which I become fully conscious of my heart's desire. If I may speak of "the method of Augustine," somewhat as Paul Valery speaks of "the method of Leonardo," I may say it is a method of coming to awareness of heart's desire through a process of recollection and prayer. Augustine's prayer in his *Soliloquies*, "that I may know me, that I may know thee," finds its answer in his *Confessions*, "you have made us for yourself, and our heart is restless until it rests in you." I come to know myself as capable of God, as desiring God, and I come to know God as the secret, the mystery of my heart's desire. The answer is already implicit in the prayer to "know me," to "know thee." As for the method of Leonardo, his motto "obstinate rigor" (*ostinato rigore*)[25] suggests that he was not satisfied with a tacit knowing of particulars. Thus his many unfinished works and studies.

I can feel in myself too an unwillingness to look away from "the particulars of my life," to "attend from" them, as Polanyi puts it, and to "attend to" the eternal in me. I can feel in myself a movement of divergence toward the particulars, equal and opposite to the movement of convergence upon the eternal. There is something destructive at work here. "Scrutinize closely the particulars of a comprehensive entity," Polanyi says, "and their meaning is effaced, our conception of the entity is destroyed." On the other hand, the particulars can be integrated again, and the meaning can be restored, and not only restored but deepened. "Motion studies, which tend to paralyze a skill, will improve it when followed by practice," Polanyi acknowledges, and "the meticulous dismembering of a text, which can kill its appreciation, can also supply material for a much deeper understanding of it."[26] That, I suppose, is the point of Leonardo's method, the spirit of the Renaissance, to study the particulars in order to comprehend better the whole. I wonder if I can use my own divergence of interest toward "the particulars of my life" in a similar way, to comprehend more fully the eternal in me.

"I would live to study, and not study to live," Bacon says in his "Memorial of Access" after saying "I am too old, and the seas are too long, for me to double the Cape of Good Hope." The Cape of Good Hope is also called the Cape of Storms. If I can weather the storms that come of studying "the particulars of my life" I can come to good hope. "I would live to study," I would live to follow my heart's desire, "and not study to live," and not struggle to live. That seems to describe the method of Augustine in his *Soliloquies*, seeking and ensuing the peace of contemplation. My heart too is capable of converging on God in me, living to study, and yet is also capable of diverging toward "the particulars of my life," studying to live. I can turn the divergence back into convergence, I can reintegrate the particulars, I can weather their storms and round the cape, like Augustine in his *Confessions*, by bringing them before God.

Here is the method I am seeking. "I would live to study," I want to say too, I would seek and ensue the peace of contemplation, but I have nevertheless to "study to live," I have to deal with "the particulars of my life," to round the Cape of Storms, in order to come to good hope. The first movement of contemplation, therefore, the one I have been considering till now, is the restless movement of the heart from one thing to another when I take it as the negative way to God, "not this, not that." The second movement, the one I am turning to now, is that same restless movement when I take it as the affirmative way, when I bring "this and that" before God in recollection and prayer. The restless movement goes on, it seems, from image to image, whatever I do, whether I am waking or sleeping, but I can find rest in restlessness, I can come to repose in movement, by the way I relate to it, living to study and thus letting it be a circling around the eternal in me, centering on the eternal, as "we all have within us a center of stillness surrounded by silence," or again, studying to live, letting myself be caught up in "the particulars of my life" and yet coming to rest by bringing the particulars before God, letting them be in God's hands.

"Do thou stand for my father," Prince Hal says to Falstaff, "and examine me on the particulars of my life."[27] I had a brief conversation once with B. F. Skinner on these words of Shakespeare. I had read a short autobiography Skinner wrote for a book of autobiographies by psychologists, and when I told him of it he said he was working on a full length autobiography. "How can you write an autobiography without a self?" I asked him, referring to his rejection of the concept of self in *Science and Human Behavior*. Looking at me with some surprise, he replied, "You write about the particulars of your life!" And indeed, when his autobiography appeared, its title was *Particulars of My Life*.[28] I didn't press him on his use of the possessive pronoun "your" or "my." But my hope now, as I go into this movement into particulars, is that I will be able to round the cape of myself and come to good hope.

Heart Speaks to Heart

"My heart speaks clearly at last,"[29] one of Tolkien's characters says in a moment of choice. Something similar could be said in a moment of renewed hope. Say I have to move from a living situation in which I have been surrounded by life and hope to one in which there seems to be no life, no hope. Say I begin to see a pattern of diminishing freedom in my life, as if I had reached a point of having fewer and fewer choices as the path narrows in front of me. Say I have therefore a feeling of dismay at the prospect of my future, as if hope

and life were being taken away, and I were surrounded by a
narrowing circle of light, until there is no horizon for me but
time and only light enough for one step at a time. I maintain
hope, insofar as I am able, by living willingly in that way, "one
step at a time out of the heart." But as I live that way, refusing
to say it is too late for me to round the Cape of Good Hope, I
ask myself what I am to do if I am to recover hope, to recover
a horizon. And it comes to me at last that there is hope for
me after all, hope in love, hope in work, and hope in the
direction of my life. I have known "the particulars" all along,
but now my heart speaks.

It is a horizon I find that gives me a renewed sense of
hope, a horizon of love, a horizon of work, a horizon that
gives a sense of direction to my life. Just as "horizonless"
is a synonym for "hopeless," as in "a horizonless grind," so
"horizon," a great circle around the particulars of life like the
great circle around the visual field, gives a sense of hopeful
orientation. It is not simply a limit, but like the visual horizon
it is a boundary that always recedes as you approach it. I see
a new horizon of love when it comes to me that there is a real
and desirable alternative for me to walking alone, there is for
me a way of spiritual friendship. I see a new horizon of work
when it comes to me that there is not only a way of words, for
instance, but also for me a way of music. And I can descry a
prospect that gives me a sense of renewed direction overall,
even when I feel "I am too old" or "the seas are too long,"
when I think of "the road of the union of love with God."

There is a horizon already, to be sure, before I come to
this new horizon of love and work, this renewed sense of
a way in life. Heidegger in the prologue of *Being and Time*
speaks of "*time* as the possible horizon for any understanding
whatsoever of Being."[30] Time is my horizon when I say "I am
too old, and the seas are too long, for me to double the Cape
of Good Hope." Time is my horizon too when I say more
hopefully "the future—any future—is simply one step at a
time out of the heart." When I speak more hopefully, though,
I have a sense of being guided, of being led by the heart,
and when my heart speaks clearly at last, not just to show me

the next step but to show me a new range of possibility, I am no longer thinking purely and simply in terms of time but in terms of eternity. Light breaks on the horizons of my mind when I recover hope, or rather I recover hope when light breaks, and eternity is perhaps light breaking on the horizon of time more than a new horizon. Time therefore can still be called the horizon but time now is transfigured by eternal presence as my way becomes a way of words and music of the heart, a way of spiritual friendship, a way of union in love with God.

What is more, when my heart speaks, when light breaks on the horizons of my mind, when it comes to me that there is hope for me after all, I am in eternal presence in the present. My relationship with eternity is not the same as my relationship with time, is not just "I and it" but is "I and thou." It is as though "heart speaks to heart,"[31] the human heart of darkness and the eternal heart of light. What then is heart saying to heart?

"When I wished to sing of love it turned to sorrow," Schubert says, "and when I wanted to sing of sorrow it was transformed for me into love."[32] Here is a hint about the way of words and music, and about the way of spiritual friendship, and about the way of union with God in love. What gives me hope when I think of these things, music and friendship and union with God in love, is a sense of possibility. "When I wished to sing of love" as an actuality "it turned to sorrow," for love is a possibility for me, "and when I wanted to sing of sorrow it was transformed for me into love," again because for me love is a possibility. What I am coming upon here, what I am entering upon, is a way of possibility: music is a way, friendship is a way, union with God in love is a way. My hope thus is not in having already accomplished something in music, not in having already achieved great friendship, not in having already attained union with God in love, but only in the way opening up before me. Living "one step at a time out of the heart," I have been praying "Show me the way!" And the answer has come, a way where there was no way.

"So I was divided between love and sorrow," Schubert goes on to say, divided between a sense of possibility, I could say, and a sense of unfulfillment. He is describing here what he calls "a dream," telling what his editor calls "an allegorical story," but one that is "founded closely on fact."[33] For Schubert too, though, the sense of possibility prevails, and his dream or allegorical story comes to a happy ending. As I contemplate the way opening up before me, I have the feeling too of being in a story where the ending is happy rather than sad. The feeling comes of this sense of possibility, of a way where it had seemed there was no way. There is "joy" here, as C. S. Lewis defines it, "an unsatisfied desire which is itself more desirable than any other satisfaction."[34] It is the joy of unfulfilled desire full of promise, the joy of newfound possibility.

When heart speaks to heart, accordingly, it speaks of possibility. As I become excited about the possibility, though, I can slip out of the heart-to-heart relation that has revealed the way of possibility to me and live just in a relation to the way itself. As long as I am in the dark, living one step at a time, my hand is in the hand of God, but when the way of possibility opens up before me, I let go of the hand of God and walk ahead confidently on my own. The way of possibility, however, is elusive as possibility itself, is not as solid as actuality, and I can lose my way as easily as I found it. To stay on this elusive way I have to stay in the relationship in which I first discovered it and in which I continue to discover it, step by step, almost as though I were still in the dark. I think of the words of M. L. Haskins quoted by King George VI,

> And I said to the man who stood at the gate of the year: Give me a light that I may tread safely into the unknown. And he replied: Go out into the darkness and put your hand into the hand of God. That shall be to you better than light and safer than a known way.[35]

When I first find the way of possibility, it seems I have found "a light that I may tread safely into the unknown," but when

I lose it again, I find living one step at a time, living heart-to-heart with God, is "better than light and safer than a known way."

Possibility can be seen as eternal, as Kierkegaard sees it, as the possibility of an eternal self, or it can be seen as temporal, as Heidegger sees it, ultimately as death, my "ownmost possibility of being at an end."[36] Living heart-to-heart with God, living one step at a time out of a heart-to-heart relation with the eternal One, I am seeing possibility as eternal. I see myself exploring the realm of music, finding possibilities there that do not die away with my death; I see myself entering into friendship that is lasting, not just "until death do us part"; and I see myself taking a road on which love and the lover live till all eternity, on which union with God in love allows me to participate in eternity. If I were to see each of these possibilities as temporal, I would see the music and the friendship dying away, the road coming to an end, my song and my story ending in my death.

To see more than temporal possibilities in song and story, I have to stand in a heart-to-heart relationship with God. There is a moment, as Kierkegaard says, when I freely enact my relationship with eternity. It is a recurring moment, a timeless point in my inner subjectivity that punctuates time again and again. "And I felt," Schubert says, "pressed as it were into a moment's space, the whole measure of eternal bliss."[37] No doubt, music dies away, my song dies away when I finish singing, and that is an image of me dying away when my life comes to an end. Composing music, nevertheless, I go through a process of discovery, as if there were possibilities in music to be discovered, possibilities that were always there and will always be there, for instance the possibilities of the pentatonic scale used in folk songs around the world, something that comes close to being a universal musical language. Moreover, in composing I am relating not just to these possibilities but to inspiration, to a kindling of my heart that illumines the possibilities and selects among them, as if God's heart were speaking to my heart.

There is some hint of God's speaking also in a spiritual friendship when one human heart is speaking to another.

There is "a breath of eternal life,"[38] as Buber says, speaking of a relationship that is "I and thou" and not just "I and it." No doubt, there is an "it" in every human relationship, even a threefold "it," according to A. T. Wright in his novel *Islandia*: there is *apia*, the attraction of one person to another; there is *alia*, what one has to share with another; and there is *ania*, the care one feels for another.[39] And all three are timebound, even care when it is limited by the boundary condition, "until death do us part." Yet friendship can survive the parting of friends; one can be present to the other even at a distance, and even in death. And it is the presence of one to another that is "a breath of eternal life."

Intimations of eternal life are strongest, though, in my very way to music and to friendship and to all else when I am living one step at a time out of a heart-to-heart relationship with God. This way of living is itself the road of union with God in love. It is "the Road" in Tolkien's song that "goes ever on." If I see my life simply in terms of my time for love and work, my road does not go ever on ahead of me, I have always less time than I did, but if I see my life in terms of knowing and being known, loving and being loved, I look forward always to more rather than less, and my road is like Georgia O'Keeffe's "Road Past the View" or like an autumn road I saw once on a friend's postcard, lined and overarched with trees and turning in the distance, disappearing into the trees. There is nostalgia in the other songs of Tolkien's song cycle, *The Road Goes Ever On*,[40] the nostalgia that goes perhaps with this vision of a road past the view, a longing for the life that has been, a delight in the life that is, a longing for the life that shall be. It is a longing that calls for music and friendship.

Still, it is a longing that can survive the ceasing of songs and the parting of friends. When that happens, the longing becomes restless again, looking for someone, looking for something. It is then especially that you feel the sense of unfulfillment contrasting with the sense of possibility, or sorrow contrasting with love, as Schubert says, almost as if peace of mind were necessary for music and for friendship. I think of Schubert composing *The Winter Journey*,[41] the song cycle of love and sorrow he wrote at the end of his life. By composing music he composes himself, as if a winter road too, like Otto Modersohn's painting of a country road in winter, were a road past the view. It is by coming back to a sense of a road going ever on, a sense of living by the heart, that I am able to compose and be composed enough to be a friend.

"Old men ought to be explorers,"[42] T. S. Eliot says and so too those on a winter journey in life, even if they are young like Schubert, exploring even as love turns to sorrow and sorrow turns to love. What brings excitement, even warmth, on a winter journey, the excitement and the warmth of a kindling of the heart, is the sense of possibilities still to be discovered, unexplored territory of the spirit. "Heart speaks to heart" in inspiration, in friendship, in divine comfort and counsel, only when I am at rest in restlessness, when I am at peace with the sense of being on a journey of discovery. "The gods only go with you if you put yourself in their path," Merlin is told in Mary Stewart's story. "And that takes courage."[43] God goes with me, kindling my heart and illumining my mind, only if I put myself in God's path, only if I let myself be led, taking things as meant, looking for signs, letting my heart speak, setting out on the way that opens up before me. And that takes courage, for the great temptation on a winter journey in life is "the combination of sublime acquiescence and irresponsible indolence,"[44] as Adorno says, the danger of giving in to an infinite resignation in which there is no hope, the danger of falling asleep in the snow.

If I can keep in touch with possibility in my life, if I can keep a sense of the road going "past the view," going "ever on," I can say "Yes!" I can come to peace without losing hope. It is possible then for my heart to speak. I think of Richard Strauss at the end of his life, writing *Four Last Songs*, and in the last one ending with the question "Can this perhaps be death?" and then answering with the transfiguration theme from his early work *Death and Transfiguration*.[45] It is as if his heart asks the question, and then he hears heart speaking to heart, not in words but in music. If I put the cry of my own

heart into words, when I am at an impasse in my life, when
it seems there is no way of possibility for me, I may well ask
"Can this perhaps be death?" Asking that, I may hope to hear
heart speaking to heart of transfiguration.

What then is transfiguration? If time is my horizon, as
Heidegger says, and death is my "ownmost possibility," transfiguration is the illumining of the human figure against this
ground when I realize I am not simply my time ("Am I my
time?"), or, reversing figure and ground, when I realize time
is full of eternity and death is full of life. Heart is speaking
to heart here as in the transfiguration of Christ, "This is my
beloved son" or "You are my beloved son," in that I have a
sense of being known and loved. Words speak to my heart;
music speaks to my heart; friends speak to my heart; and my
own heart speaks. All this conveys a sense of being known and
loved. Or it does when I am at peace, when I am accepting of
my time and my death. But if I am striving against time and
death, if I am looking for someone or something, if I lack
"sublime acquiescence," the willingness I need to combine
with my hope, then I find myself coming to words and to
music with a kind of desperation, coming to friendship out
of emptiness rather than fullness. Then it becomes difficult
to let words or music speak to the heart, to let the heart speak
in friendship or in discerning the way.

Figure and ground can be reversed by striving and again by
willingness and hope, luminous figure against dark ground
becoming dark figure against luminous ground, and vice-
versa. I think of Arnold Schönberg writing *Transfigured
Night*, where love is transfigured like death, where love is
a dark ground, a night that becomes luminous, and then
later writing *Pierrot Lunaire*, a song cycle in an atonal style,
where moonstruck love is parodied, where the human figure becomes luminous but with a strange moonlight. "Paler
indeed than the moon ailing in some slow eclipse was the
light of it now," as Tolkien says of his bewitched tower of the
moon, "wavering and blowing like a noisome exhalation of
decay, a corpse-light, a light that illuminated nothing."[46]

There is a hint of magic here, of true and false transfigu-
rations, of true dreams and visions coming through the Gate

of Horn and false dreams and visions coming through the Gate of Ivory. When I am waiting on a friend to call, but to no avail, when I am waiting on someone or something more intangible, on God, on an illumining of the mind, a kindling of the heart, but again to no avail, I am tempted to make a choice like the one proposed by Pindar, "O my soul, do not aspire to immortal life, but exhaust the limits of the possible."[47] I am tempted to give up on the thing that can only be a gift, the friendship of the friend, the illumining, the kindling that is of God, to give up on "immortal life," and instead strive to "exhaust the limits of the possible." Imagination is the faculty of possibility, and I am tempted to live in imagination rather than in the heart, to live in that strange moonlight, that reflected light that comes from an imagination separated from the heart. I am tempted to transfigure human relations with my imagination, to be led by dread and fascination rather than to wait on the deep stirring of the heart.

It is cold, living in the imagination rather than in the heart, cold as the theological student turned composer finds in Thomas Mann's novel *Doctor Faustus*, selling his soul to the devil in exchange for twenty-four years of musical genius. "Cold we want you to be, that the fires of creation shall be hot enough to warm yourself in. Into them you will flee out of the cold of your life," the devil says. "And from the burning back to the ice. It seems to be hell in advance, which is already offered me on earth," the composer replies.[48] There is a better way, it seems, another way to create, rather than living in the imagination, and that is living in the heart, and letting heart speak to heart, and letting possibilities be revealed to me that I have not imagined. I can enlarge the limits of the possible, it seems, by aspiring to immortal life, to gift rather than to theft or to exchange.

"Exchange, gift, and theft," Roland Barthes says, "the only known forms of economy."[49] All three, it seems, are economies also of the imagination: discovery or *gift* and appropriation or *theft* and substitution or *exchange*. If "I'm outside my heart, looking for the way back in," if I have been living in my imagination rather than in my heart, the two ways of theft and exchange are of no avail to me because they keep me within the realm of imagination, taking something from here and putting it there, replacing one thing with another. Only the way of gift, the way of discovery, takes me beyond the realm, beyond to its source in the heart. Perhaps it is just the willingness to receive, to let a gift be given me, that is enough to take me there to the source. I am "looking for the way back in," and perhaps this is the way. I am tempted to exchange my soul, "immortal life," for the imaginative genius to "exhaust the limits of the possible." So if instead I open my soul to "immortal life," if I allow my heart to "aspire" to it, I will find my way back into my heart, the seat of life and light and love.

If I do aspire to immortal life, I am led on a journey into the imagination of the heart, like that Hermann Broch describes in his novel *The Death of Virgil*, where he envisions not just a life after life but a deeper life lived now that is able to live on through and after death. Broch's novel (which he began writing in a Nazi concentration camp) takes us on a journey through water, fire, earth, and air, the elements symbolic of human experience, a coming, a going, a waiting, and a homecoming of the spirit. It is a journey to the sources of imagination in heart and soul. My hope now, as I begin this last movement of contemplation, passing into the imagination of the heart, is that I will be able to pass through the heart of darkness and come to the heart of light.

Following the Heart

"And never was the earth nearer the heart of light," Broch writes, "nor light closer to the earth than in the approaching dusk at the two boundaries of night." At sunrise and sunset, the two boundaries of night, at birth and death, the two boundaries of life, light is nearest to the earth, he is saying, the heart of light is nearest to human existence. So if I want to find my way, I can go to these twilight borders of life, back to birth in recollection, forward to death in anticipation, hoping for a flash of insight arising from a sense of my life as a whole, like Virgil in the story, at the boundary of sunset, at the boundary of death. As he lay dying on a ship approaching shore at sunset, Virgil's hands were quivering, reaching and grasping for the growing things of earth, as "the longing fear" of his hands became "a mighty endeavor,"

> an endeavor to hold fast to the unity of human existence, to preserve the integrity of human desire in a way that would protect it from disintegrating into manifold existences, full of small desires and small in desire; for insufficient was the desire of hands, insufficient the desire of eyes, insufficient the desire of hearing, sufficient alone was the desire of heart and mind communing together, the yearning completion of the infinity within and without, beholding, hearkening, comprehending, breathing in the unity of the doubled breath, the unity of the universe.[50]

Thus, on his entrance into the concentration camp, feeling his own "longing fear," Broch describes the heart's desire.

I feel a "longing fear" too when I approach the boundaries of my life, when I think back to birth, when I think on to death, a longing for the unity of the universe in the unity of my life, a longing for "simplification through intensity," as Yeats says, and a fear of "dispersal."[51] The simplicity, the intensity, will come of following the passion of my life, following the heart's desire. It will come of "creative imagination through antithetical emotion," as Yeats calls it, imagination in the service of the heart, not just raw "primary emotion" but "antithetical emotion" or "the desire of heart and mind communing together." Dispersal, on the other hand, "disintegrating into manifold existences, full of desires and small in desire," comes of a fear of loss, a fear of missing out on life, and that fear can lead to "enforced self-realization," as Yeats says, living out the many and small desires.

So if "I am outside my heart, looking for the way back in," I have to turn from divergence to convergence. It seems easy to get outside my heart but hard to find my way back in, easy to go in the direction of divergence, to be "full of desires and small in desire," but "a might endeavor" to go in the direction of convergence and unity of life. If I am on the right track, though, in saying it is not a matter of striving but of willingness and hope, then finding my way back into my heart is a matter of discovering the direction of convergence where it already exists in my life and going with it. Alfred Adler's saying, "the unconscious is the direction we are not looking,"[52] is a guide here. I have to look in the direction I have not been looking. Say I have been looking to the future, expecting the future to be like the past, but have come to a point where there is no more hope of it being like the past, and am left therefore simply looking to the past. If I look deeper then into the past, I may be able to look deeper into the future. "What seest thou else in the dark backward and abysm of time?"[53]

Asking myself again that question Prospero asks of Miranda, I find myself looking for some deeper pattern in my life, as if I were looking for some unifying theme in a complex piece of music, something that can carry through from the past into the future and give my life its unity. What leaps to mind now, as I write of "Love's mind," is an unknowing love of God. All through my life I have been in love with God, if that is the theme, mostly without knowing it but with glimpses of knowledge and awareness. Can unknowing love be the direction of a life?

An unknowing love can lead us on paths that go nowhere without thereby wasting our life or our time, for all our life and all the time we have been in love. I am fascinated with the thoughts that come of going nowhere or of facing a dead end, for that is when an unknowing love can become knowing. Edward Elgar in his last years, saying "my wife is dead, my friends are dead, my music is dead," decided to go on a voyage up the Amazon.[54] Broch's Virgil was tempted to burn the manuscript of the *Aeneid*. There is the temptation to repudiate a past that has left one without a future. To find the deeper pattern, the theme of one's life, is to find a current that runs deep in the seemingly still waters of time past and time future, something that is going on even when everything seems over, something too that is the source of what more evidently has happened in a life, a creative force inspiring love and work and yet failing at times to prevent destructive things also from happening. The love of God is just that, it seems, especially an unknowing love of God. It is an inexhaustible source of inspiration, and yet, unknowing as it can be, forsaken in times of fear and despair.

Imagining life beyond death is something we do in facing death but also in facing a dead end in life, and the love of God is something that can emerge in that imagining. I think of Virgil imagining the afterlife in Book VI of the *Aeneid* and again in Broch's novel, and I think of Dante journeying through the afterlife in *The Divine Comedy* with Virgil as his guide and how he ends with "the love that moves the sun and the other stars," and I think of Newman imagining the after-life toward the end of his own life in *The Dream of Gerontius* and of Elgar setting Newman's poem to music. The love of God is essentially the link between this world and the other world. Without the love there is a break in continuity and life divides into this life and the afterlife, and the afterlife seems imaginary rather than real.

To "realize," I read once in a dictionary, is to "imagine vividly." But "vividly" comes about when "the passion of your life becomes more vivid," as Forster said, speaking of the effect of music. Only as love of God, it seems, can the passion of my life pass through death, only as love of God can it pass through the dead ends of life. When it is a dead end I am facing, say a living situation I would not have chosen, a situation I am in against my will, I imagine a kind of half-life, a life of gradual disintegration, but when I remember the love of God, the half-life gives way to the prospect of a fullness, of a living that is loving. When it is death I am facing, then too I imagine a sort of half-life, the life of a ghost, or perhaps no life at all, but when I remember the love, I think of living until death parts us, and when I remember the love of God, I think of living on and loving on, I think of the enduring passion of an eternal life. And whether it is death or simply a dead end I am facing, I imagine vividly, I *realize* the passion of my life.

I imagine a continuity of passion from this situation to the next, from this life to the next, and imagining it I realize it, at least from one situation to another in this life. "I know I am traveling all the time," as Lundkvist says from his hospital bed, making "journeys in dream and imagination," but as the passion of my life becomes more vivid I realize these journeys. They become for me what Dante's journey through the other world became for him, "high fantasy" (*alta fantasia*) and yet really being "moved by the love that moves the sun and the other stars." They become for me what his meeting with Beatrice was in the other world, "the meeting in dream,"[55] as Borges calls it, and yet the real meeting of "all real living is meeting," the reality of a human relationship. They become for me what Dante's were for him, the matter of song, "a guiding song" like the song Broch's Virgil hears on the ship approaching shore, "for only the serene may guide."[56]

"A guiding song," that is what I am looking for when I am facing death, when I am facing a dead end in life, a song that is serene, "for only the serene may guide," and yet a song to rouse the passion of my life. On his deathbed Saint Thomas Aquinas asked that the Song of Solomon be read to him, the Song of Songs as it is called, a love song really where God is not mentioned, but to Aquinas a song of the love of God. For me too, "a guiding song" may be a love song, a song of passion, but to me a song of the love of God, a song of serenity. When I am facing death, against my ownmost will to live, when I am facing a dead end, against the forward movement of my will in life, I know the secret of serenity is what Dante says, "his will is our peace" (*la sua voluntate e nostra pace*), but as I align my will with God's will, I find I am aligning my will with my heart's longing, I find my will has not been the same as my heart's desire, I find the direction I have not been looking. It turns out that God's will for me is not simply my acceptance of death, my coming to a dead end, but rather the direction I have not been looking, the direction of my ownmost longing.

I find the direction by embracing the situation I have not chosen, by "choosing necessity,"[57] as Helen Luke says, not simply acquiescing in it with resentment. I am able then to uncover the possibility of the situation, to find the way of possibility in what is seemingly closed necessity, and the resonance I feel in myself with this way, this possibility, shows me or assures me it is the direction of the heart. There is matter of song here. There are two elements in poetry, according to Max Jacob, "style or will and situation or emotion."[58] By embracing the situation rather than simply acquiescing in its necessity I let it affect my style or will, but in the embracing the emotion gives way to the deeper resonance of the heart, "and when I wanted to sing of sorrow," as Schubert says "it was transformed for me into love."

"And once a pious maiden who had just died appeared to me," Schubert goes on to say, describing his dream in a way that is reminiscent of Dante meeting Beatrice or Novalis meeting his beloved Sophie in the other world. "And a circle formed about the tomb in which many youths and old men wandered as though in perpetual bliss."[59] When I choose necessity, when I embrace even death itself, I become free and the way of love opens before me. "I longed to walk there too," Schubert says, to join the circle of love beyond death, ". . . and before I knew it I was in the circle, from which the loveliest melody sounded." There is a danger here, to be sure, of "the combination of sublime acquiescence and irresponsible indolence" Adorno speaks of in Schubert's and Berg's last days. In this dream of Schubert's, though, I see only the "sublime acquiescence" and not the "irresponsible indolence," I see the freedom towards love that comes of freedom towards death. "And I felt, pressed as it were into a moment's space, the whole measure of eternal bliss," Schubert says, like Dante describing Paradiso after his reunion with Beatrice beyond the grave.

Freedom towards love, that is what comes of choosing necessity, of accepting even death. It is something real, a real capability of love, even though it is enacted in imagination as in Schubert's dream. By casting aside resentment and actually choosing the situation that is imposed on me by circumstances I become able to love. Imagination comes into this as the faculty of possibility, envisioning the way of possibility. Resentment, long lasting, deep marked by indignation and smoldering ill will, is the thing that stands in the way, darkening the heart, blocking love and imagination. When I let go of resentment, I do not immediately come to love but to its possibility, to "journeys in dream and imagination." My openness to love, nevertheless, allows love to enter into my life, allows me to live clear down in my heart.

There is a reconciliation in this choosing of necessity. I am passing from a conflict with my situation to a consent that resounds in my heart and is an embracing of the will of God as I understand it. I am passing really from a conflict of wills to a union of wills. Schubert saw a reconciliation with his father in his dream. "My father I saw too," he says, "loving and reconciled. He folded me in his arms and wept. And I still more."[60] I am seeing a kind of Gethsemane here. "My Father, if it be possible, let this cup pass from me; nevertheless, not as I will, but as thou wilt," Jesus says in the Garden of Gethsemane, and then later, "My Father, if this cannot pass unless I drink it, thy will be done."[61] There is a conflict of wills, mine and God's, when I encounter an inescapable situation that is against my will, and then a reconciliation when I embrace the situation, choosing necessity. I am coming to a heart according to the heart of Christ, but I go through a hell, like Dante, as I feel the conflict, and then a purgatory, as I pass from will to willingness, letting go of resentment, and I come at length to a paradise where I am able to say with Dante, "his will is our peace."

A saint is one who is "in bonds to truth: and in that bondage," Helen Waddell says of W. P. Ker, "the humanist who died on a mountain top at the age of 68, joyously and vigorously pursuing the freedom of his own will, was content to serve."[62] One can be "in bonds to truth," she is saying, and yet "joyously and vigorously pursuing the freedom of his own will." Perhaps that is the real meaning of "his will is our peace," not a renunciation of will but a bondage to truth. It is a bondage that allows for the joyous and vigorous pursuit of the freedom of your own will. Indeed when I *choose* necessity, I am in an active stance of will and choice rather than a passive one of resignation, and so in that very act of "sublime acquiescence" I am pursuing the freedom of my own will "joyously and vigorously," saying "Yes!" to God's will.

It is John of Salisbury, secretary to Thomas Becket, who said the saint is one "in bonds to truth," and that brings to mind Becket's fear in facing martyrdom, "to do the right deed for the wrong reason," and the chorus of demons mocking Gerontius with their question "What's a saint?" and Broch's Virgil in his dark moments of self-doubt accusing himself of "perjury" and of "breaking the pledge of creation."[63] All of this is like Pilate's question "What is truth?" and is met by silence, though all through the Gospel of John it has been answered by "I am," the expression of the presence of God. To be "in bonds to truth" is to be in the presence of God, to live in the presence. "We all have within us a center of stillness surrounded by silence." To live "in bonds to truth" is to live in that center of stillness surrounded by the silence of God's presence. But those challenges "What's a saint?" and "What is truth?" come on a journey where we are passing from exhaustion to a lack of will or of desire, to a resignation, to a willing and choosing acceptance where we are reconciled to our lives and we are happy. Short of that reconciliation, that happy light, it can seem we are living in untruth. To see the light coming is to see in the dark.

"Those ages had need of the Virgilian tenderness, the language of the heart,"[64] Helen Waddell says of the Dark Ages, and you could say that also of the dark moments of exhaustion, of lack of will and desire, of resignation, on the way to reconciliation and peace of heart. They have need of tenderness like Virgil's, the language of the heart, for it is that tenderness, that language of tenderness that makes the heart articulate, that enables you to see in the dark, to see light with your heart when all your eyes see is darkness. There is a direction running though those dark moments that does not want to stop at exhaustion, at depressed lack of desire and will, at resentment and resignation, but is always heading towards the moment when all will be engulfed in love. To choose necessity, it seems, is the act immediately preceding the moment when love reigns, but love itself is the direction leading to love.

Love's direction is the way of possibility; love's consummation is in union or reunion. "But for our human griefs, for the last Virgilian tenderness," Helen Waddell says of poetry in the Dark Ages, "read Alcuin writing to the friend of all his life . . ."

> No mountain and no forest, land nor sea,
> Shall block love's road, deny the way to thee . . .
> Yet why must love that's sweet
> So bitter tears beget . . . ?

Love's road is love's direction and goes ever on and on, but union or reunion can seem always out of reach. That is why "when I wished to sing of love it turned to sorrow," and yet "when I wanted to sing of sorrow it was transformed for me into love." Alcuin goes on to speak of eternal life as union or reunion, and not only with God but with the human beloved:

> And thou, my heart,
> Make haste to fly
> Where is delight that fades not,
> The unchanging shore,
> The happy house where friend from friend divides not,
> And what he loves, he hath for ever more.
> Take me, beloved, in thy prayer with thee,
> Where shall be no estranging thee and me.[65]

If we were to speak of eternal life as love's direction, though, we could say it begins already with our first steps on love's road. It is everlasting, as love's road goes ever on and on.

My heart's desire, my hope, my willingness, these are the three things that come to light on love's road, and these are the answers to the question with which we began, "What does the heart's desire look like in the mirror of death, in the

magic of transfiguration, and in the mystery of eternal life?"
In the mirror of death the heart's desire looks like the restless
movement of the heart seeking a love that is intimate and yet
lasting. In the magic of transfiguration, however, the heart's
desire is kindled and illumined with hope as heart speaks
to heart and the way of possibility opens up before me, the
way of words and of music, the way of spiritual friendship,
the way of union in love with God. And in the mystery of
eternal life the heart's desire becomes willing as I choose
necessity, following the heart in situations with such a will
that a way appears where it seemed there was no way to union
or reunion. *Love's road is the way of the heart's desire.*

"Thou art the journey, and the journey's end," King Alfred
concludes in prayer, answering the darkness of the Dark Ages
not "in logic, but in excess of light."[66] It is an answer also to
the dark times in which we live and to the dark moments
we encounter on love's road, to think of the journey as a
journey with God as well as to God, to think of God as the
heart's desire. "God is my desire," I am saying with Tolstoy,
when I say "Thou art the journey, and the journey's end,"
and saying this is poetry in dark times. I like the title of
Helen Waddell's lecture, *Poetry in the Dark Ages,* for poetry
understood as "the language of the heart" is "a guiding song"
for us in dark times and in the dark moments of our journey
in time, "for only the serene may guide." As I follow the
guidance of "the language of the heart," realizing my heart's
desire is "not this, not that," knowing it is love I long for,
intimate and lasting, finding hope in the way of words and
of music, the very language that is guiding me, finding hope
also in the way of spiritual friendship where love is lasting if
not intimate, finding hope in the way of union in love with
God where lasting love becomes intimate, I choose necessity
and embrace the situations of my life as love's road.

If I follow love's road, letting myself be guided by the
language of the heart, I find myself being led towards a
union or reunion that cannot be fully described even in that
language. "It was the word beyond speech,"[67] Broch ends,
telling of the endpoint Virgil comes to in facing death, as if

following the way of words and of music leads to something beyond speech, to something nevertheless that has to do with words and music. I think of the Gospel of John, "In the beginning was the Word." Broch is saying "In the end was the Word." There is a long stretch of love's road nonetheless that is the matter of story and song, that can be told or sung in the language of the heart, a long stretch of road where "a guiding song" can still guide.

Meanwhile there is a presence in language, a presence of "the word beyond speech," especially in the language of the heart. "We can know more than we can tell," especially when we are telling of love's road. It is this untold presence that enables "a guiding song" to guide, the peace of this presence, "for only the serene may guide." I find this serenity, this presence, for instance in *Ancient Voices of Children*,[68] a song cycle, words of Garcia Lorca, music of George Crumb. I can feel the serenity, the presence, in the words of the songs, "The little boy was looking for his voice," "I have lost myself in the sea many times," "From where do you come, my love, my child?" "Each afternoon in Granada, a child dies each afternoon," and "My heart of silk is filled with lights." I can feel it also in the dances that come in between, but it becomes explicit only in the final words of the last song, the "creative germ," as the composer says, the "original impulse" of the whole work, "and I will go very far . . . to ask Christ the Lord to give me back my ancient soul of a child." I want to ask that same thing now. I want to learn how the friends of God become lovers of God.

The Lovers of God

"my ancient soul of a child"
— Federico Garcia Lorca

There is a desire in all our desires, I believe, an enthusiasm in all our enthusiasms. It is an unknowing love of God. It is what I may call "my ancient soul of a child." To hear that love in all our loves is to hear "ancient voices of children," and I may have to go very far along love's road to know it and to love with a love that is knowing. I hear those voices in the love of words and in the love of music and in the love of friends. I hear a child's love of the unknown in my fascination with words and in the other world I enter in music and in the mysterious life I share with a friend. It is an unknowing love, but it is unknowing like "the cloud of unknowing in the which a soul is oned with God."[1]

As love becomes more knowing, or more knowingly "unknowing," as I learn to discern the love of God in all our loves, I become more peaceful about love not being consummated in possession, about the words I love not being mine, about the music I love not being mine, about the friend I love not being mine alone. It is consummated rather in being "oned with God" who belongs to all, who is "mine own, and not mine own." My unknowing, the "cloud" of my unknowing, is darkest at this point. I do want the words to be my own; I do want the music to be my own; above all, I do want the friend to be my own alone. I want possession. I think of the image of "The Beguiling of Merlin" on the cover of A. S. Byatt's romance *Possession*[2] and the hint that to possess is also to be possessed. To let go of all that, to let

83

the words and the music I love be those of others, to let my
friend be a friend of others, is possible for me only when I
am at peace, only when I am living in my center of stillness,
surrounded by a silence that feels like a presence, only when
I have a sense of being "oned with God."

To possess and be possessed is the counterfeit of being
"oned," the false over against the true consummation of love.
But to be "oned with God"? Is that what we are seeking? Is
that what I am seeking? "Love is of such a nature that it
changes us into the things we love,"[3] as Meister Eckhart says,
and that is what happens in the love of words, the love of
music, the love of friends. Words become my life; music becomes my life; friendship becomes my life. I come into touch
with the mystery of words, with "the word beyond speech"; I
begin to live in that other world I discover in music; I begin
to participate in the mysterious life I see in my friend, to live
that life myself. Yet being "oned with God" is something still
more pure and simple. It is being in the peaceful center of
silence and stillness where words and music come from; it is
being where friendship comes from and goes to in my life.

I hear "ancient voices of children" when I go into my own
center of stillness, the voices of feelings I did not realize
I had. "Late have I loved you, beauty so old and so new,"
Augustine exclaims in his *Confessions*, "late have I loved you."[4]
Late, because the beauty is so old, like ancient voices, and
yet so new, like the voices of children. In fact, it is the voice
of a child, singing "Take and read," that leads Augustine into
his realization. How am I to listen to my own voice of a child,
"my ancient soul of a child," to come to my own realization
of love?

Remembering Love

"I have passed through fire and deep water, since we
parted," the sage says in Tolkien's story. "I have forgotten
much that I thought I knew, and learned again much that
I had forgotten."[5] There is a passing through fire and deep

water, I find too, after the parting of friends, there is lack
and loss and letting go, and there is forgetting, letting go of
notions I had entertained, letting go of sadness, and there is
remembering, becoming aware of my real feelings, becoming aware of love I never really knew I had. "Your father
loves you," the sage says further on, "and will remember it
ere the end."[6] There is such a thing as remembering a love
that has been forgotten. I realize I am loved and I have been
loved all along; I realize I do love and I have loved all along;
I remember love. What is more, passing through fire and
deep water, through the pain of loss, I realize there is a love
in all our loves. I have known this. I have known it without
knowing I knew it. And now I come to remember, to know I
knew, to know I know of love. "All love is lost but upon God
alone," or when all is lost love begins again with God.

"I felt—therefore I was,"[7] F. Scott Fitzgerald said in a time
of emotional exhaustion, remembering that he had once felt
but not being able to feel again in that memory. To feel
again, to recover the inspiration I have lost, it is not enough
to recall having had feeling, to recall having had inspiration.
I have rather to wait on a more substantial memory that
actually brings love back to me. I have to wait on what is
essentially an involuntary memory. I have to wait, I want to
say, on God. When I remember in this more substantial way,
feeling comes back to me, inspiration comes back. It comes
to me as a gift. It enables me to love. It is the kind of memory
Proust discovered for himself in his *Remembrance of Things Past*
when the mere taste of a madeleine brought the past back
to him and filled him again with joy. When all is lost, I wait
on God and some simple occasion is able to revive me.

Waiting on God, I am adding something to what Proust
says of remembrance. It is not a matter of applying more
energy to thinking, of trying harder to remember, but of
directing thought to a different point of origin, of directing
thought from memory to God. When Augustine directs his
thought to memory in his *Confessions*, he doesn't find God,
he says, but only when he directs his thought to what is above
his mind and memory.[8] It is in the stance of prayer that his

memory becomes alive for him. For Proust too, trying to remember doesn't bring the past to life, but the seemingly accidental encounter with some reminder. "Attention is the natural prayer of the soul," and the orientation towards God in prayer is an attention to what seems accidental or incidental in present experience. It is an attention that does not allow the accidental or incidental to pass unnoticed, an attention that takes everything that happens as somehow meant to be. Proust practices that attention without calling it "the natural prayer of the soul." To call it "prayer" or "waiting on God" as I am doing is, I think, to name the tacit dimension in remembrance. *Is the love of God simply attention, the natural prayer of the soul?*

It is "connatural" for us, according to Aquinas, "to love God above all things."[9] Is the connatural love of God the same as the natural prayer of the soul, I am asking, and is attention the secret of the remembrance of things past? I may risk spoiling remembrance by trying to make the process conscious. If I take prayer simply as attention and take attention simply as prayer, though, I do not spoil remembrance, I think, but make it easier. Let us see what happens if I take the love of God simply as attention, and take attention simply (or not so simply) as the love of God.

"Attention is the natural prayer of the soul" is a saying that goes back to Malebranche in his *Conversations*, and is repeated by Walter Benjamin in his essay on Kafka, and by Paul Celan speaking of poetry.[10] "Even if Kafka did not pray— and this we do not know—he still possessed in the highest degree what Malebranche called 'the natural prayer of the soul': attentiveness," Benjamin says. "And in this attentiveness he included all living creatures, as saints include them in their prayers." It is an attentiveness that reaches to all beings like God's own love or like that of a saint calling all living creatures brothers and sisters. It is the kind of attention you give to the persons who belong to your life, remembering them every night in your prayers. "The attention which the poem pays to all that it encounters, its more acute sense of detail, outline, structure, color, but also of the 'tremors and hints,'" Celan says, quoting the saying, "—all this is not, I think, achieved by an eye competing (or concurring) with ever more precise instruments, but, rather, by a kind of concentration mindful of all our dates." It is an attention that goes with mindfulness of time, with time in memory, even with a search for God in time and memory.

It is especially when I meet with something that is against my will, a situation I would not have chosen, that my attention becomes a search for God in time and memory. In fact, attention becomes prayer when it is directed not just to the person or to the situation I meet but to the light in which I can understand our meeting. Here is what Malebranche actually says. "The attention of the spirit is the natural prayer we make to the truth within," he says, "so that it will discover itself to us."[11] It is attention to what the Quakers call "the inner light," the divine presence in the soul that gives spiritual enlightenment and moral guidance and religious assurance. Malebranche himself is speaking the language of Augustine in his *Confessions*, seeing everyone and everything in time and memory in the light of divine truth dwelling in the soul.

"But this sovereign truth does not always respond to our desires," he goes on to say, "because we don't well know how we are to pray."[12] When a situation is against my will, it is very hard for me to see it in the light of a higher truth. I have to let go of my own will in the matter to practice attention as a prayer of the soul. I am like the child Samuel learning to communicate with God. It is as if everyone and everything were calling me by name or as if God were calling me by name on every occasion, but I have to go like the child Samuel from saying "Here I am!" pointing to myself, to praying "Speak, Lord, for thy servant hears,"[13] opening myself to what is greater than myself. I think of Saint John of the Cross when he was in prison, definitely in a situation against his own will, and how he heard a song being sung outside in the streets, a love song,

> I die of love, my dear,
> what shall I do?
> —Go on and die![14]

He was moved to ecstasy and began to write his own love
songs with their well-known darkness, their night of sense
and of spirit. He was dying anyway and he took the song he
heard as a call to turn his dying into loving, to turn death
into love. Eventually he escaped from his prison cell, and he
took his escape likewise as a freeing of the spirit, a freeing
that comes of accepting death in love.

Maybe this is the deeper and darker meaning of involuntary memory, the kind of memory Proust found so life-giving.
It is a memory that comes of letting go of my own will, of
passing from will to willingness. It is only when living in a
room that is not according to his own taste, not arranged
according to his own will, Proust says, that he feels fully alive
and thinking. "I leave it to people of taste to make of their
rooms the very image of their taste, and to fill them only with
things of which they can approve," he says. "As for me, I feel
myself living and thinking only in a room where everything
is the creation and the language of lives profoundly different
from mine, of a taste opposite to mine, where I find nothing
of my conscious thought, where my imagination is excited
by feeling itself plunged into the depths of the not-me (*non-
moi*)."[15] There, it seems, is the secret of this involuntary
process of coming to life, to be plunged into the depths of
what is not me.

I am building a bridge here from the aesthetic to the
mystical, from Proust to Saint John of the Cross. As I consider
my own experience of living in a situation against my will, I
can see that crossing the bridge, from Proust's room to Saint
John's cell, is a matter of conjoining Saint John's faith, or his
hope, if you will, with Proust's willingness. It is a faith in love,
a trusting in the love of God to lead me through the dark
night of unknowing. There is a poem of Saint John's where
he speaks the language of unknowing, very much as in *The
Cloud of Unknowing*. It begins

> I entered where I know not
> and stayed there not knowing,
> all knowledge transcending.[16]

Where? I am in that situation against my will, but it is transformed now by my trust in the love of God leading me "where I know not."

What can I know?
What should I do?
What may I hope?

Kant's three questions.[17] I can ask them now as I face this situation against my will with willingness and hope. Can I know without knowing what I can know? Will I be able to act without knowing what I should do? May I hope without knowing what I may hope? Yes, I can, I will, I may in this cloud, this dark night of unknowing, trusting in the love of God to guide me and guard me.

I enter "into the darkness with love," as the anonymous author of *The Cloud* says, and thus I "choose necessity" and my will is in this matter that is against my will. The unknowing love of God pervading my life, not the same as my will, becomes knowing or knowingly unknowing, as will comes into accord with love. Unknowing love is love that goes further than knowing takes in, but now I am beginning to take it all in. I am "living and thinking," as Proust says, in this situation where things are not in the image of my taste, where they are not arranged according to my will. I am "plunged into the depths of the not-me," but I do not really lose me in "not-me," I come into accord rather with what is deepest in me, my heart's yearning, deeper in me than my will or my taste, I come into accord with my heart's desire for union or reunion.

"Do not go gentle into that good night," Dylan Thomas writes in a poem to his father going blind, "Rage, rage, against the dying of the light,"[18] and that is the counsel I have to follow to save me from "not-me," from being spiritually destroyed by it. I have to maintain my will in the face of a situation against my will. Therefore I submit my will not to the situation itself, not to another human will, but to the inner light of the heart's desire and to that inner light

alone. The direction of my will, of my attention, becomes
thus the direction of love itself, the love of God. And the
"inner light" becomes the "kindly light" Newman sings of in
his song "Lead, kindly light." It becomes the light of love,
the love of God illumining the entire landscape of my life.
If I were to submit my will to the situation against my will
rather than to the inner light, a kind of blindness would
come over me, a numbing of the heart, and it can come over
me anyway when I am in such a situation if I lose touch with
the inner light. "But this blind dark seems to be getting into
my heart," Frodo says to Sam on Tolkien's epic journey in
the Dark Land. "As I lay in prison, Sam, I tried to remember
the Brandywine, and Woody End, and the Water running
through the mill at Hobbiton," he says, naming places he
loves. "But I can't see them now."[19]

Here is the spiritual danger of living in a situation against
my will. "Do you remember . . . ?" Sam asks further on in the
story. "No, I am afraid not, Sam," Frodo replies. "At least, I
know that such things happened, but I cannot see them."[20]
All the things I love become abstract memories, "At least, I
know that such things happened," but I cannot bring back
the living memory, "I cannot see them," I cannot bring back
the love. It is because there is a kind of numbing violence
in the situation against my will. I can overcome it only by
looking in the direction I am not looking, by looking to
the inner light, by bringing the situation to the light. The
very thought of being in a relationship with the inner light,
however, takes away the sense of isolation there is in simply
being in a situation against my will. It is as if nothing else
matters, if I have a sense of being led by the kindly light.

To remember love is first to look in the direction of love,
and only then to remember the things I love. The direction is
that of the darkness and the light, the darkness of unknowing
and the light of heart's desire. It is the direction of light
leading in the darkness. It is towards mystery. Say I feel very
restless inside and completely unable to fix it. I can't even
distract myself very well. I can't find home. I feel lonely, as if
everyone but me had found love that is lasting and intimate,

everyone but me had found union or reunion. When I do
calm down and just sit in the darkness of unknowing and
of unfulfilled desire, I know it is not really the unions I see
of others that I long for, it is something more, and only by
being pushed this far into the darkness am I truly forced to
calm down. Things can feel wrenching inside until I open
up to the darkness and go with it. But the peacefulness that
comes of yielding is a relief like no other. Little by little, my
sense of joy is returning and I am coming home in spirit.
I am remembering love. I am yielding not to the situation
really but to the light shining in the dark, I am yielding to a
darkness that is also light.

There is an excitement I feel, drawn by mystery, drawn
to the mystery, on the road into the mystery, "the road of
the union of love with God." Everything comes back to me
now, my old loves, my old enthusiasms, as if they were all this
love, this enthusiasm. I am excited because now it seems this
road I have been on is going somewhere after all. My fear, I
realize now, was that it was a path leading nowhere, that all
my loves, all my enthusiasms, would come to nothing. "All
love is lost but upon God alone," but now it seems all love is
love of God somehow and so no love is lost. All my loves, all
my enthusiasms, belong on the road of union in love with
God, and so all of them serve to carry me forward in love.
"Everything which belongs to an individual's life shall enter
into it,"[21] I can say with Jung, and I can add, "Everyone who
belongs to an individual's life shall enter into it."

As I remember the persons who have entered my life, as
they enter my mind again, I find my way back into my heart
again, and that is how I know they belong to my life. My being
out of my heart goes with them being out of mind, like "time
out of mind." It is true, the persons of my life transcend my
life and have lives of their own, and letting them transcend
my life, letting them have lives and cares of their own, letting
them be, is not easy, letting go of them really and being
thankful for them. Still, I can tell the story of my life by telling
of the persons of my life, as Marcus Aurelius does at the beginning of his *Meditations*, mentioning the principal persons

of his life and being thankful for what each of them gave him. "Courtesy and serenity of temper I first learnt to know from my grandfather Verus," he begins. "Manliness without ostentation I learnt from what I have heard and remember of my father. My mother set me an example of piety and generosity. . . ."[22] An so on through grandparents, parents, a sister, a brother, teachers, comrades, kinsmen, friends, and last of all, the gods. I can speak of the persons of my own life in this way, and I can call them "those whom thou hast given me," as if to say they themselves are the gift given to me.

Letting the persons of my life transcend my life, letting them have an independent existence, letting them have lives and cares of their own, means my becoming heart-free and heart-whole. It means freedom for me from the past and openness of my life to the future. Maybe that is the ultimate meaning of the saying I have been quoting, "All love is lost but upon God alone." It comes from a poem by William Dunbar at the beginning of the sixteenth century, "The Merle and the Nightingale." The Merle, the blackbird, that is, sings "A lusty life is in the service of love," a life full and fulfilled, that is, but the Nightingale sings "All love is lost but upon God alone,"[23] and so they go on, back and forth, until the Merle at last agrees with the Nightingale, and they fly away.

Remembering love is remembering God, I conclude, keeping God in mind. It is "emotion recollected in tranquillity." Remembering God, I mean, allows me to recollect emotion in tranquillity rather than in a way that is wrenching inside. "Poetry is the spontaneous overflow of powerful feelings," Wordsworth says: "it takes its origin from emotion recollected in tranquillity."[24] Here again I am building a bridge, this time back from the mystical to the aesthetic. Love as a direction, I am saying, a direction of living and thinking towards God, makes it possible to remember love as a state of soul, to recollect emotion and yet to recollect it in tranquillity. As I remember the persons of my life, my feelings towards them come back to me, and I have to let the persons be, to let them belong to my life and yet transcend it, if my feelings for them are to be "emotion recollected in tranquillity." If I do not let them be, if I do not let go of them really, I let go instead of my tranquillity, of my peace of mind. If I can let them belong and be in my life and yet transcend it and have their own lives, I am able to love them without losing my own peace and freedom of heart.

My loves, my enthusiasms, as they come back to me in recollection, are purer for this tranquillity than they ever were in their time. And if I come out of such recollection to "the spontaneous overflow of powerful feelings," I am taking a new step on love's road. Old relationships that were broken off can come to life again, and when they do, in the midst of letting be and letting go, the relationships come to life as pure gift, as grace from God, so it seems, as if my letting be and letting go were answered with "those whom thou hast given me" in the language of the Gospel of John, as if to allow me to say in those words, "Of those whom thou gavest me I lost not one."[25] It is as Kierkegaard always hoped, thinking of Abraham giving up Isaac and receiving him back, by giving up those dearest to me I receive them back again.

Remembering love, if love comes to life again in this way, is not just "recollection" but "repetition," as Kierkegaard says, or since love is purer when it comes to life again, not just "repetition" but "realization." To be sure, I am tempted to fall back into love as it was, to desire possession, longing to possess and be possessed, but if I stay with the peace of love "recollected in tranquillity," of love renewed and repeated in tranquillity, of love realized in tranquillity, I begin to walk along love's road. And in that peace of mind I learn what it is to love "with all your heart, and with all your soul, and with all your might." I learn what it is to be "oned with God." I learn "purity of heart is to will one thing." Proust speaks of the experience of being "incapable of willing" and how "What is necessary, then, is an intervention which, while coming from another, takes place in our innermost selves, which is indeed the impetus of another mind, but received in the midst of solitude."[26] He is talking, it is true, of what may happen in reading, but it is just what happens in remembering love.

There is grace in remembering love, "an intervention which, while coming from another, takes place in our innermost selves." Aquinas too, after saying it is "connatural" for us "to love God above all things," goes on to say nevertheless in our fallen human condition we need "the help of grace healing nature"[27] if we are to love God above all. Just reading can be the occasion of grace, reading scripture like Augustine, reading a book like Proust, reading the letter of a friend. Whatever the occasion, something "takes place in our innermost selves." I remember love, feeling comes back to me, and in remembering the past, I find myself on love's road into the future. Instead of love being a thing that has passed from my life, I find love's road goes on into the unknown.

Love's Road

"Blue soul, dark road,"[28] Georg Trakl says in a poem, as if to say the darkness of the road goes with the blueness of the soul, blue perhaps as in the Blue Rider watercolors by Kandinsky meant to suggest the element of the spiritual in art. The "dark road" is death's road. It is the road of life seen as leading to death. No doubt, there is a coming to life, a coming to live more fully, when your life opens up before you all the way to death, when you realize you will die someday. It is an intensity of life, like a blue flame, and that perhaps is the meaning of "blue soul," a soul intense with life, burning like a blue flame, an intensity that is also simplicity, a simplicity that is also intensity. The Blue Rider in Kandinsky's watercolors seems almost to fly, and we can imagine riding along this dark road with an intensity that is almost flying, an intensity that becomes luminous, a luminous blue, and illumines the darkness of the road, changing it from death's road into love's road, or revealing in the light of this blue flame that death's road is in reality love's road. For the intensity and the simplicity of this blue flame is that of spiritual love.

Then again the darkness of the "dark road" is perhaps that of unknowing, and the intensity of the "blue soul" illumines the road into the unknown. When I remember death, *memento mori*, I remember love, I come to life and light and love, and the intensity and the simplicity of that energy somehow clarifies the direction of my life. Say I have been living in uncertainty about my way, about words and music and friendship in my life; say I have been thinking about the passing of time; say I have been wondering about where to go with words and music, where to go with friendship; say I have come back again and again to the thought of living "one step at a time out of the heart." Is there a step, though it is only one step, that will set me moving again on love's road?

"No mountain and no forest, land nor sea, shall block love's road, deny the way to thee..." Alcuin wrote to his friend. May I say that to a friend? May I say it to God? Not without adding what follows, "Yet why must love that's sweet so bitter tears beget...?" Still, it is something to affirm love in the face of separation. It is like affirming life in the face of death. It is like affirming light in the face of darkness. It is the step I have to take to set me moving once more on love's road. I think of the poetry of Saint John of the Cross, how it begins with an affirmation of love in the face of separation and ends with an affirmation of union or reunion with God. Or so it does in "Dark Night" and "Spiritual Canticle," poems on which he wrote prose commentaries. In a third such poem, "O Live Flame of Love," the affirmation of love and the affirmation of union or reunion are one and the same except for a thin membrane separating the lover and the beloved, and he asks "come through now please break this sweet encounter's web." May I say that to God? Stating the thesis of his fragmentary essay, *A Lover's Discourse*, Roland Barthes says "the lover's discourse is today of *an extreme solitude*" and yet "it has no recourse but to become the site, however exiguous, of an *affirmation.*"[29]

Reading one of Saint John's poems every night before sleeping, as a friend has suggested, I am trying to move from my own "extreme solitude" to "an affirmation." Reading can seem a very tame thing to do, but then I think of Proust calling it "a communication in the midst of solitude." That is what I may hope now, reading the poetry of Saint John, a

communication in the midst of my own solitude, a communication from a greater purity of heart, a greater intensity, a
greater simplicity, a communication really from God, heart
speaking to heart, an illumining and a kindling.

"Blue soul, dark road" seems at first to describe Saint
John's poetry of love as well as Trakl's poetry of death. "The
stranger's out on the road, ahead of everybody else," Heidegger says, commenting on Trakl's poetry. "He isn't just
wandering about, with nowhere to go. All the time, he's
coming closer to the place he can call his own."[30] Indeed
when my life opens up before me to death, when I remember
death, I feel like a stranger on the earth, I feel "an extreme
solitude," for it seems to me I have my own death to die and
nobody else can die it for me. I feel already in advance the
loneliness people feel on their deathbed, as if I were dying
while everyone else goes on living. My loneliness can reach
also into the realm of love, as it seems to me in the face
of lonely death I am not first in anyone's heart, I have my
own death to die, my own life to live. To pass from such "an
extreme solitude" to "an affirmation" is indeed—to come
closer to a place I can call my own. That place in Trakl's
poetry, according to Heidegger, is "apartness" where to be
alone is to be all one, but in Saint John's it is union or
reunion in love, and "the road" is "of the union of love
with God."

To be apart or to be one again in love, that is the difference. I feel always a desire to follow my heart in life and yet
a fear I will have to walk alone. I know I will be at peace if I
follow my heart, but just hearing the voice of another person,
of someone I believe in and trust, is sometimes enough to
allay my fear, to bring me hope, to restore my faith that even
if I have to walk alone I will end up in something more than
just aloneness. I think of the story *Not First in Nobody's Heart*,
the story of a Chippewa man and his search for love. I think
of how it ends not in his being first in someone's heart so
much as in someone being first in his heart. "She will always
be first in my heart"[31] he says of the woman he finds to love
and then loses to death.

"It is by loving, and not by being loved," George MacDonald says, "that one can come nearest to the soul of another."[32] I emerge from the extreme solitude of being "not first in nobody's heart" by letting someone be first in my heart. That is my affirmation, "I love" rather than "I am loved." In Saint John's poetry I emerge by letting God be first in my heart, but there too, though God's love is greater than our love, and God therefore is nearer to us than we are to ourselves, loving us more than we love ourselves, the affirmation is of our love. The poetry is not about us being first in God's heart but about God being first in our heart. Is our love of God really so great as that? Is Saint John's love so great as that? It is very striking that in his poetry he always wears the mask of a female lover. All the references to himself in the poems are in the feminine gender in Spanish. These are perhaps allusions to the female lover in the Song of Solomon, the song echoed in all of these songs. Are they also perhaps the mask of a greater love, a greater purity of heart, into which the poet wishes to grow?

That is what they are to me, these feminine guises, a "mask," as Yeats uses the term in *A Vision*, an image into which I am seeking to grow. For Saint John himself, though, they may be simply the truest expression of his own love, a "mirror," as Yeats says, more than a "mask." Still, in the language of the Renaissance, in the usage of Saint John's times, that is just what a "mirror" is, an image into which you may grow. There is an insight latent in this way of speaking. By growing into the love of God you are growing into your own true heart's desire. By wearing the mask of a great lover, you gain access to the great love that is latent in your own heart. You hold up a mirror to your self that reflects what you can only call "the face I had before the world was made."[33]

Now let me try and translate the poems of Saint John myself from the Spanish,[34] not all of them but those describing the "blue soul" and the "dark road." First, the one on the "blue soul," for it touches on the great love latent in the heart, the guiding principle on the "dark road." It begins

O live flame of love,
so gently hurting
at deep center in my soul!
since you hold back no longer,
come through now please
break this sweet encounter's web.[35]

There is indeed something "gently hurting at deep center in my soul." Can it be this "live flame of love"? If so, do I dare ask it to burn through the "web" that separates us and consummate our "sweet encounter"? The poem goes on,

O gentle burn!
O easy wound!
O tender hand! O subtle touch
that savors of eternal life
and pays off all I owe!
By slaying you've changed death to life.

O lamps of fire
whose splendors
in deep caves of sensibility,
once dark and blind,
give warmth and light together,
strange and lovely for the loved One!

How tender loving
you awaken in my heart
where secret and alone you dwell;
and in your breathing sweet
and full of good and glory,—
how carefully you make me fall in love!

If I just let the poem itself speak to my heart, without turning to the prose commentary and letting it speak to my mind, I am able to appropriate what is said in the poem, to connect it with my own experience of the heart's longing. That longing is not clear to me by itself, for it is aroused by remembering death as much as by remembering love. This poem, though, "O Live Flame of Love," allows me to take my heart's longing as the "live flame of love" and to

take its ascendancy in my life to mean I am in love with
God and have been in love even before I knew I was in
love. That gives me hope in the face of my own death, for
it means my life is not just about living and dying but about
loving and about loving God and thus about something that
is not ephemeral, something that is eternal, something that
is capable of surviving death.

I can turn now to the prose commentary simply by translating the title given to the poem, a summary of the commentary in prose: "Songs of the Soul in the Intimate Communication of Union of Love of God."[36] What it says to me
is that this poem is about something more than my heart's
longing, something that is more like the consummation of
my longing, the intimacy of communication with God in
the soul's union or reunion with God in love. That pushes
me away from the poem. At the same time, nevertheless, it
draws me on with the thought of something yet to attain,
something to hope for, something to live for beyond what I
have already known. Then again, I wonder how I was able to
read the poem simply in terms of my heart's longing. It may
be because union with God is not something other than the
love of God. It is "union of love of God," *unión de amor de
Dios.* And it may be because the heart's longing becomes the
love of God. That is what happens on "the road of the union
of love with God," *el camino de la unión del amor con Dios,* the
longing becomes the love. What is said of the love can be
said also of the longing.

What happens then when longing becomes love? There is
then "the intimate communication," *la íntima communicación,*
that is spoken of in the poem's title. As I understand it, there
is a kindling of heart, and the kindling becomes in turn
an illumining, of heart and of mind, heat becomes light,
and that kindling that is also an illumining, that heat that
is also light, is felt as an "intimate communication," heart
to heart, divine to human heart and human to divine heart.
But the kindled heart is the heart in love with God and that
is none other than the heart longing for God. It is a subtle
difference, this between the love and the longing, between

the love of God and the heart's yearning, and yet it can be a long journey to go from longing, just longing, to love, true love, and a great transformation for longing to become love.

Now let me try to translate the poem about that long journey, that great transformation, that "dark road" of longing and how it leads to love. It begins

> In dark night
> with longings kindled into loves
> — O lucky venture!
> I set out unseen,
> my household now at rest.[37]

My translation, "with longings kindled into loves" for *con ansias en amores inflamada*, may reflect my own thoughts here about longing and love and the kindling of the heart. There is excitement, nevertheless, at the very thought of setting out, and setting out on such a high adventure as this. The poem goes on,

> In darkness and in safety,
> by the secret ladder, in disguise,
> —O lucky venture!–
> in the shadows and in hiding there,
> my household now at rest.
>
> In the lucky night,
> in secret so nobody saw me
> and I saw no thing,
> with no light no guide other
> than that burning in my heart.
>
> It guided me
> more sure than noonday light
> to where awaiting me
> was someone I knew well,
> there where no one appeared.

It is a "dark road," longing for what I do not know and coming to know more and more clearly who it is that I desire. The enlightening thing here is the excitement itself, the

hope, the kindling of the heart that comes with being on
"the road of the union of love with God." My heart's longing
without such an exciting hope is only a wistful yearning. With
this hope it becomes a passion—fulfillment is possible! What
is its fulfillment to be? The poem concludes,

> O guiding night!
> O night more lovable than dawn!
> O night uniting
> love with loved one,
> changing her into her love!
>
> Against my flowering breast,
> all kept for him alone,
> he lay asleep,
> and I was fondling him,
> and fanning cedars gave a breeze,
>
> The castle air,
> as I played with his hair,
> and he with his serene hand
> touched me on my neck,
> and put all of my senses in suspense.
>
> I lay and I forgot,
> my face reclined upon my love;
> all ceased and I let go,
> leaving my care
> among the lilies out of mind.

Here too I can turn to the prose commentary simply by
translating the title given to the poem, "Songs of the Soul
that Rejoices at Having Attained to the High State of Perfection, That Is Union with God, by the Road of Spiritual
Negation."[38] And here again I see what I have missed in the
poem itself, "the road of spiritual negation." It is the road of
letting go of everyone and everything and becoming heart-
free and heart-whole. Is it not possible, though, to be heart-
free and heart-whole without being in love with God? I think
of Martin Heidegger talking about *Gelassenheit*, "letting be"

or "releasement toward things."[39] But then again he is talking
about thinking, not about loving. He is mind-free not heart-
free. To be truly heart-free and heart-whole then is to be in
love with God? Yes, it does seem so, letting be and letting
go, leaving everything behind, comes of the enthusiasm of
setting out on love's road. It is the excitement you can feel
in the poem, the kindling of heart on this high adventure,
that enables you to let go of everyone and everything and
set out on this long journey into night.

It is a twofold night, according to the prose commentary, a
"night of sense" and a "night of spirit."[40] It is like the twofold
nightmare Conrad describes in *Heart of Darkness*, a nightmare
of soul and a nightmare of soullessness, for me a passing
through the darkness of my own heart, through the darkness
of longing and fear where longing has not yet become love,
my nightmare of soul, and through the darkness of spiritual
desolation where I do not feel the excitement of love's road,
my nightmare of soullessness. "In a real dark night of the soul
it is always three o'clock in the morning,"[41] F. Scott Fitzgerald
says, describing his own nightmare of soullessness. I suppose
the point of going through these things is to bring light and
warmth into these dark and cold corners of the heart. It is
learning to love with all your sense, and with all your spirit.

That is it, learning to love, that is what these dark nights
of the soul are about, learning to be whole in love, sense
and spirit. Is the love of God then simply attention, the
natural prayer of the soul? That is the question with which
we began. When I pray, when I direct my thinking and living
to God, I can feel the darkness of my longing and my fear,
I can feel my lack of feeling when the excitement of love's
road is not there. "Love is a direction, and not a state of
soul," Simone Weil says, but the direction makes me very
aware of the states of soul, and the direction carries me, it
seems, from one state of soul to another. It is true, love is
not simply a direction I give to my living and thinking but
a direction I find already there at work in my life. When I
go with it, when I let it become the guiding direction of my
life, it becomes conscious and willing. It becomes a light in

the darkness of my heart, and I find myself living "with no light no guide other than that burning in my heart." *Attention becomes conscious love of God when the natural prayer of the soul becomes conscious prayer.*

As I meditate again on the words of the old man of the desert to Lawrence, "The love is from God, and of God, and towards God," I can see that love's direction, the *from* and *of* and *towards*, as it becomes conscious and willing, is the hidden meaning of my life and my times, even of all life and time. "I am scattered in times whose order I do not understand," Augustine says in his *Confessions*. "The storms of incoherent events tear to pieces my thoughts, the inmost entrails of my soul, until the day when, purified and molten by the fire of your love, I flow together to merge into you."[42] That is what becomes the vision of his *City of God*. I find myself now being led to such a vision, meditating on my own life and times, as he did on his, and seeing how the kindling of my heart on the adventure of love's road leads to an illumining of my mind in vision.

"I am scattered in times whose order I do not understand." I feel like saying that too when I read a newspaper, and see how the Four Horsemen of the Apocalypse are at large, war and famine and pestilence and death, and how humanity is divided by hatred. "The storms of incoherent events tear to pieces my thoughts, the inmost entrails of my soul," I want to say with Augustine too, "until the day when, purified and molten by the fire of your love, I flow together to merge into you." I want to be caught up in the love that is "from God, and of God, and towards God," and I want to see everyone and everything caught up in the love, flowing together and merging into a reality that is from and of and towards God. Thinking this way, I don't mean to say simply that everything is made of everything else and that things do not have their own structure. I mean rather that the real structure of things, the very inscape of human lives as well, is this love from and of and towards God. I touch upon this inscape, I believe, when I am in touch with heart's desire. I touch upon it in others when heart speaks to heart.

There is a duality here, but not a dualism of equal and opposite forces. It is a duality I find in myself, as Augustine found in himself, of knowing and unknowing, of loving and unloving. The dark nights of the soul, the "night of sense" and the "night of spirit," are the times of passage through unknowing to knowing, and through unloving to loving. As I see it, the key of passage is devotion to prayer, to attention, to love of God as the conscious prayer of the soul. The passage is from simple attention to love, from natural prayer to conscious prayer. As I remember death, I remember also love, and there is an intensity of feeling and of life in the face of death that becomes love. I think of *Harmonium*, a composition for chorus and orchestra by John Adams, setting the poem "Negative Love" by John Donne to music,

> If that be simply perfectest
> Which can by no way be express'd
> But Negatives, my love is so.
> To All, which all love, I say no.
> If any who deciphers best,
> What we know not, our selves, can know,
> Let him teach me that nothing; this
> As yet my ease and comfort is,
> Though I speed not, I cannot miss.[43]

That is how I feel, passing or trying to pass from longing to love. If anyone can decipher our heart's longing, can know our selves as we ourselves do not, then "let him teach me that nothing," that no-thing, "not this, not that," that I long for without knowing what I want. As it is, I must go through this unknowing to knowing, I must go through this unloving to loving. Meanwhile my restless longing is "negative love," a longing that loves "not this, not that" and I wait for it to become a longing that openly longs for God, that openly loves God. "The poem really is about the humility of love," Adams says, "and my response was to see it as a kind of vector, an arrow pointing heavenward."[44] For myself, I see I must stay with the humility of a longing that is becoming love, a longing that is as yet "negative love," and let it become for me a vector pointing along love's road, an arrow from God and to God, pointing in love's direction, "from God, and of God, and towards God." As long as I am moving in love's direction, I can conclude with the poem,

Though I speed not, I cannot miss.

Love's Mind

"no answer in logic,
but in excess of light"
— Helen Waddell

"Tell me about love," I said in my dream. "Do we love with a love we know or with a love we do not know?" And the answer came, "With a love we do not know." Now, after thinking about it and discussing it, I believe we were talking about the heart's longing. It is a love we do not know, but it is something we can feel, something moreover that can guide us in choosing our way in life. It is our key to understanding the love of God, for the longing becomes the love. It is our key really to understanding whatever we can of God at work in our lives and times, for the longing itself is at work in our lives and times as an unknowing love, a "negative love."

An unknowing love at work in our lives and times could be mistaken for an unloving knowing at work in the conflict of purpose and cross-purpose, something like Hegel's "cunning of reason."[1] You could see in ethnic conflicts, for example, where one particular cause is set against another, the means by which some universal principle such as that of democracy comes about to resolve the conflict, and so likewise in religious and intellectual conflicts. You could see the principle itself of science, of democracy, of ecumenical religion, as a kind of knowing that wins out through the opposing loves and hatreds of particular views, of particular causes, of particular ways of life. I want to look instead to the wholeness of the individual human being, transcending all causes and principles, and to the heart's longing that springs up in that

107

wholeness and guides the individual towards fulfillment. I see all human beings standing in a circle, as it were, the "human circle," each located somewhere on the circle by particular circumstances, "the particulars of my life" as Shakespeare calls them, but each one drawn towards the center of the circle by the heart's longing.

Love's road for each of us is a radial path from the point on the circle where particulars locate us to the center where we may hope to find our heart's desire. The radial paths converge on the center. So the further we go on our own paths the closer we come to one another. We are heading toward a vision like Dante's at the end of his *Divine Comedy*, a great golden rose of human beings converging on God. I suppose the thing that has come into light for us since Dante is the thought of these radial paths to the center, a thought that traces the convergence of his vision all the way back from eternity into time. Just as he himself passed through hell and purgatory and heaven during life on earth, so we too find in time the paths of eternity. Still in time, like Dante "lost in a dark wood" or like Shakespeare's lovers lost in "a midsummer night's dream," we find it is hard to discern true paths from woodland paths leading nowhere.

It is these woodland paths leading nowhere, as it seems, these "firebreaks" or "lumberjack trails" (*Holzwege*), that may lead us, according to Martin Heidegger, toward the "clearing" (*Lichtung*) of our own existence.[2] They can be paths of "negative love," I surmise, paths of a heart's longing that cannot be satisfied with someone or something we have set our heart upon, paths that lead us therefore to insight. They lead "nowhere" in that they lead to no fulfillment, but they can lead us to a moment of enlightenment in which we come to know our own heart. They lead into a "clearing" that is a "lighting" of our life. There are "deserted cities of the heart"[3] in this wilderness, like the abandoned cities of the Yucatan, realms where once our heart was dwelling, where someone or something once was dear to us. These "deserted cities of the heart," I think, are what we find in the "clearing," in the "lighting" of our life. When we come upon these places, we may remember love and find love's road again, not so much to live in these deserted places again, but to guide our heart toward the place we are seeking, the city of the heart where we can find heartsease.

"In the forest clearing to which his circular paths lead, though they do not reach it, Heidegger has postulated the unity of thought and of poetry," George Steiner says, "of thought, of poetry, and of that highest act of mortal pride and celebration which is to give thanks."[4] When I come upon the deserted places in my heart, the places where once I lived, I am taken with regret and with fear, with regret at lost opportunity, with heartache, with anguish, even remorse, and with fear that comes in part from the heartache of this regret, fear of the known as well as of the unknown, of the experienced as well as of the unexperienced. If I can give thanks for what has been, if my thinking can become thanking, as in the saying of the seventeenth-century mystics, "Thinking is thanking" (*Denken ist Danken*),[5] then I am able "to cast aside regret and fear" and move forward on love's road, for thinking and thanking means letting go of what has been and being open to the mystery of what is to come.

Is there a city of the heart? I ask myself as I contemplate these "deserted cities of the heart." Is there a city ahead on love's road, I mean, or only these deserted cities I leave behind? There are times when I feel very alone on the road I am following, but I do have nevertheless a sense of being "guided and guarded" as Tolkien says, when my heart is in my journey. That must be the essential condition, that my heart be in what I am doing, for when my heart is elsewhere, wandering along roads I have not taken, or when it seems to me life is elsewhere, with someone else, with something else, I do not feel the guiding and the guarding. It is only when my heart is here on the road taken that I feel it, for then I seem always to find friends who belong to my life, I seem always to find situations that open up before me and point the way ahead, I seem always to find my heart speaking or coming to speak clearly at last, I seem always to find a way where there seems to be no way. I am guarded as long as I stay with the guiding I receive, but when my heart is wandering, looking for someone or something, I become more vulnerable to destructive encounters.

As long as I stay with the "inner light," bringing every situation to the light, as the Quakers say, and bringing the light to every situation, I feel "guided and guarded," and the light, as I understand it, is the light of the kindled heart, of longing become love, "no light, no guide other than that burning in my heart," and the heart, as I understand it, is not just the seat of emotions but the center we each have within us where thought and feeling meet, "a center of stillness surrounded by silence." By entering into my own center of stillness and aligning it with the center on which all the paths converge, I take a sighting on my own radial path, on my heart's desire. And the heart's desire, as I understand it, is not an object I find at my center or even at the center of convergence so much as a direction from center to center, from heart to heart, a love that is from and of and towards God.

My purpose is to be moved by that love, like Dante at the end of his vision, moved by "the love that moves the sun and the other stars,"[6] to be moved by it, to be led by it step by step along my own radial path to the center. Being moved by that love is at once loving and being loved, at once knowing and being known. Passing from Dante's universe of concentric spheres to ours of spiral galaxies and black holes, I feel the shifting of images while pivoting on the insight that carries over from one image to another. It is true, in our image of the universe there is "the infinite immensity of these spaces," as Pascal says, "that I do not know and that do not know me."[7] It is possible, nevertheless, to go into this darkness too with love and not just retire from it into an inner world. It is possible to "rekindle hearts in a world that grows chill,"[8] as Tolkien says, to find a path of the heart's desire even in this universe, no longer human-centered, in which we live. The thought of being "guided and guarded," the thought of being even a friend of God, brings warmth into this cold, light into this darkness. I find myself invoking the light, invoking the warmth, the "kindly light," to find my way.

It may be that music without words is a way of imaging this universe that is no longer human-centered, music without words, or as in Salieri's ironic motto, "First the music, then the words," the title of a comic opera he wrote, *Prima la musica, poi le parole.*[9] Salieri is a fascinating figure, Mozart's rival and thus an image of failure, and yet Beethoven's teacher and Schubert's. Pure music, or "music alone," that has so flourished in modern times, may indeed be a way we have found of coming into a human relationship with a world that is not human. For me, to be sure, the way of words has been primary, has been the road taken, and the way of music has been the road not taken that only in later years has rejoined the road taken and then as music with words, song cycles, as if I were trying always to image a universe that is human-centered after all.

I see now that I have something essential to learn from pure music, namely how to relate humanly to a universe that is not human or not entirely human. All the same, I *have* learned something, how "the passion of your life becomes more vivid," as E. M. Forster says, something that is common to music with and without words. Voices that speak in poetry, "the three voices of poetry," as T. S. Eliot calls them, the voice in soliloquy, the voice in colloquy with an audience, and the voice in colloquy with other voices in a play, all can speak from the heart and to the heart, and all of them can become the voices of memory speaking to us in solitude, speaking of the essence of things. We can come to relate humanly to the universe, I mean, by way of words and music. We each have a song, I have learned, just as we each have a story, a song that may remain unsung and a story that may remain untold. If we sing our song, however, we give expression to our heart's desire, we enact our human relationship with a universe that is not human and we enter into a to-and-fro with the universe that is human for us.

"Music and poesy use to quicken you,"[10] Shakespeare says, to enliven you, to kindle your heart, and conversely, we can say, the song is the expression of the person quickened, enlivened, of the heart kindled. Improvising, we find our own song, our own relationship, our own way to the center.

A spell, a prayer, a formula, "Must it be? It must be! It must be!" "O Lord, let something remain," "I walk alone," my song puts me on my radial path to heart's desire. "Some books are forever sealed within their first utterances," Carlos Fuentes says: " 'It was the best of times, it was the worst of times' . . . 'Call me Ishmael' . . . 'I know I am traveling all the time.' "[11] So it is with a person's song, the heart's desire is sealed within its utterance. "Purity of heart is to will one thing." A personal song is linked with purity of heart, with willing one thing, and comes to expression as that one thing comes to light, as that willing comes about, as we come to be heart-free and heart-whole.

What then is our human relationship with a universe that is not human? It is a relationship of time, it seems, of time and eternity. Because our lives are in time, we are in the world, but because we are not just in time but also in eternity, we also somehow transcend the world. Time is mysterious, "a changing image of eternity," a human experience that we use nevertheless to measure a universe that is not human. Asking himself what time is, Augustine says, "if no one asks me, I know," and then goes on to speak of singing a hymn, Saint Ambrose's hymn, "God creator of all."[12] There is a connection here. When reading becomes "divine reading," *lectio divina*, letting words speak to the heart, and when reading changes into singing, as Proust says, and the way of words becomes the way also of music, then the past becomes present, becomes as Proust describes it "the Past familiarly risen in the midst of the present," and something more than the past comes to light, something timeless, eternity itself, and time gives way to heart's desire. I think of Augustine's own hymn about our restless love of "this" and "that." It is all we have left of his poetry, three lines quoted in his *City of God*. It is an evening song to be sung at the lighting of the candle,

> These goods are good because they are by you,
> and nothing ours is in them but our sin
> of loving them by you instead of you.[13]

It is as if time were to give way to eternity, and restlessness to rest, at the lighting of the evening candle. There is "letting be" in these words and "openness to the mystery." But there is one phrase in Augustine's last line that I could not get into my blank verse translation, and that was *ordine neglecto*, "order neglected," meaning love's order bypassed. Our sin, according to Augustine, is essentially one of bypassing love's order, "loving them by you instead of you." In fact, he goes on to say "love's order" (*ordo amoris*) is almost a definition of virtue. Our heart's longing, as it moves restlessly from one thing to another, has not yet discovered love's order. That comes only with rest in God, repose in light, and it means loving God in all and all in God. Still, there is a process of coming to rest in God, of coming through restlessness to rest, it seems to me, that we can see in Augustine's life and that seems essential also to love's order.

Say I believe "our heart is restless until it rests in you" but I feel in myself all the same a restless movement from one thing to another, from one person to another. It is a restlessness not of will but of desire, moving not from one reality to another but from one image to another. So rest is still possible, a rest of the will, as in "purity of heart is to will one thing" and in "his will is our peace." It is a rest of will in a restlessness of desire.[14] As I understand it, this is a willing acceptance, a consent, a Yes to a heart that is restless until it rests in God. That willing acceptance, that consent, that Yes to my own unquiet heart, brings me into my own center of stillness surrounded by the silence of God's presence, or I take that silence to be presence surrounding me when I am in my center. I am quiet then in unquiet, at rest in unrest, like a spinning gyroscope or a turning balance wheel, resting in the restless movement of my heart, as if it were as vital as my heartbeat, and taking its movement from one thing to another to be "negative love" that says "not this, not that."

"We listen to our inmost selves," Martin Buber says, "and do not know which sea we hear murmuring."[15] Is it a sea of human longing? Is it a sea of divine love? It is a vast expanse certainly, an overwhelming flood, an agitated surface, unquiet and yet capable of calm and of being transparent to its depths. Perhaps we are encountering inside ourselves the same vast expanse we encounter outside in a universe that seems no longer human-centered. By coming to our center of stillness then perhaps we come also to the center of the universe, or we enter into that direction of love that goes from heart to heart, from one center to another. Listening to our inmost selves, we hear our own murmuring heart and we hear the murmuring heart of the universe. The direction we are looking, or listening, is that of our will—we have chosen to listen—but it is also the direction of love, from and of and towards God, and of inner peace.

Heart speaks to heart then when "we listen to our inmost selves," even though we "do not know which sea we hear murmuring." I listen to my inmost self and I don't know if I hear God speaking or my own heart speaking. But even if it is my own heart that I hear speaking it may nevertheless be God speaking, for God leads us by the heart. Likewise when I am waiting for insight, I am waiting on God, but I am waiting also on my own heart, waiting for my heart to speak clearly, for instance, when I have a choice to make. "Let me think!" says one of the characters in Tolkien's epic. "And now may I make a right choice, and change the evil fate of this unhappy day." Then, after a moment, "My heart speaks clearly at last. . . ."[16] So it is, when my heart speaks clearly at last, I take it to be God speaking, and so too, when words speak or music speaks to my heart, I take it to be God speaking. Taking it that way is a way of relating to my own heart, letting myself be guided by the "inner light," the light of the kindled heart, letting the light be enlightenment and guidance and assurance.

It is when things seem to go against my heart's desire that I feel most of all my need of an enlightening and guiding and assuring light. Are things going against my heart's desire, I ask myself, or are they only going against my will? It is hard to tell, especially when they go against the freedom of my will, when they cut back my freedom of choice, I mean, for then they are clearly against my will, but because they are against my freedom to follow my heart they seem to be against my heart's desire as well—I think again of the man "who died on a mountain top, joyously and vigorously pursuing the freedom of his own will." Following the heart in these circumstances means following the inner light, letting it put my situation in perspective, letting it guide my choice of response to my situation, and letting it assure me God is with me after all.

"Humility is endless,"[17] T. S. Eliot says, and so is the heart's desire, lasting through all the separations of the will. By always rejoining the human race, each and every time I meet with a reverse to my will, I am able always to find again the way of the heart. It is like finding a path in a forest damp after rain, a trail that is difficult to make out. You cannot seem to find it by close scrutiny, and you have to look away for a moment and rest your eyes, and only then look back again, with fresh eyes now, to discern the path. I cannot seem to find the path in the direction I have been looking, the direction of my will, and so I have to look away and then look back again, in the direction I have not been looking, and there find the way of the heart. When I have to give up my will's direction, it feels like humility, and there seems no end of the number of times in my life when this seems called for, always another time, as if humility were indeed endless. This humility, of letting go, of looking away, of looking back again, allows me to pass from the high road of the will to the low road of the heart's desire.

I know, in the song "You take the high road and I'll take the low road," the high road is the road of the living and the low road is the road of the dead. Indeed, letting go of my will and its direction can seem a kind of death, but following the heart's desire and its direction can seem a kind of love, a love of God, and here I come upon a hope where there seemed to be no hope. I remember love, as if I had forgotten it in the pursuit of my freedom of will. I remember someone I love, I remember something I love. Feeling comes back to me where I had lost all feeling, and hope comes too where I had lost all hope, the hope of someone or something to love, to live for, where it seemed I had no one and nothing to love, to live for. I remember love and I live again. I remember God and the love I remember seems to be the love of God.

Remembering love, feeling again my feeling for someone or something, can mean remembering God, feeling again my heart's longing. For it is not just a state of soul that returns but a direction that is the essential direction of my life. When I have forgotten that direction, my life becomes chaotic. It is like arriving somewhere late at night with no one to meet you, where time is ahead of or behind the time you have come from, and finding nowhere to stay but a room by yourself. The loneliness, the disorientation in time, the depressed feeling, is like losing touch with the direction of your life, like forgetting what is essential. Remembering love, remembering God, is remembering the essential, remembering your way and your goal. "I remember, I remember, the house where I was born," Thomas Hood says in a poem where each stanza begins "I remember, I remember."[18] That is the kind of excitement you feel. I remember love, I remember God—feeling comes back, not just image, and direction comes back, not just feeling. Remembering love, remembering God is not just remembrance of things past. It is eternal recollection.

As I bring to mind the eternal, I say "I'll take the low road," the road of love and death, the low road of the heart's yearning. Still, it is no more death's road than the high road of the will, that of the man "who died on a mountaintop, joyously and vigorously pursuing the freedom of his own will." Letting go of my own will, I am like Dante at the beginning of his journey, giving up the attempt to climb directly to the hilltop when he sees the leopard, the lion, and the wolf waiting for him there, and taking instead the guidance that is offered to him, the shade of Virgil sent to him by Beatrice, his love remembered, leading him by the low road of hell and purgatory to paradise.[19] I wonder if I should not be "joyously and vigorously pursuing the freedom of *my own* will." But maybe that is just what I am doing, pursuing freedom on the low road itself, learning to be heart-free in love.

That is it, *to be heart-free in love*, that is what I am learning in this dark night that comes upon me in the thwarting of my will. But "to be heart-free in love" can seem a contradiction in terms, for "heart-free" usually means "not in love." So to be heart-free in love, according to this, would mean to be and not to be in love. As I understand it, nevertheless, being heart-free means letting be and being in love means being open to the mystery. So it is possible to let someone be, to let something be, and at the same time be open to the mystery dwelling in that person or thing. Letting be is my free act of will, releasing someone or something from my own expectations, while being open to the mystery is my willingness to let it speak to my heart, to let heart speak to heart. Being in love usually means being caught up in the fascination of the mystery, I know, but being open to the mystery can be intense too, and it is more, it is a relatedness that is freely chosen. Love's road, as I learn to be heart-free in human love, becomes for me the road of divine love, "the road of the union of love with God."

Bringing love to mind, I come to love's mind, I come to the city of the heart. There are places in the heart where I no longer dwell, "deserted cities of the heart," and there are "places in the heart which do not yet exist," as Leon Bloy says, "and into them enters suffering that they may have existence,"[20] and there are places where my heart dwells, far away from where I am now, as in Tolkien's story, "Were I to go where my heart dwells, far in the North I would be wandering in the fair valley of Rivendell."[21] The city of the heart is where I am when I am living clear down in my heart, living all the way down in my heart, that is, and living clear, bringing love to mind, coming to love's mind. And so the city of the heart is no merely private place, for all human hearts dwell in that same solitude. It is like the city of Augustine's vision, the city of God, where heart speaks to heart, the peaceable kingdom where we may hope "nation shall speak peace unto nation."[22]

There is a kind of universality about matters of the heart, I am saying, that makes communication possible, communication and communion. "Deserted cities of the heart," places in my heart where I used to dwell, are also lost cities of the mind, where living and thinking came together, places of refuge, while reading a favorite book for example, where I could find a sense of vision and peace of mind. "Places in the heart" that I discover through suffering, through love lost and found, through intimate love that does not last, or through lasting love that is not intimate, are also occasions of insight, of the learning that comes of suffering, that comes of lack and loss and letting go. And "where my heart dwells," where I would rather be when I find myself in a situation I would not have chosen, is a direction that can illumine the darkness of the situation in which I find myself, "a light to you in dark places," as Tolkien says, "a light when all other lights go out," a beloved and guiding image I am to keep in mind, and afterwards "when the memory of the fear and the darkness troubles you, this will bring you aid."[23]

There is always something of the mind in these matters of the heart, a peaceful vision in times of trouble, a learning that comes from suffering, a light when other lights have gone out. And this something of the mind is love's mind. Martin Versfeld has said of Augustine, and particularly of his vision of the city of God, that his lifework was "to kindle the light of things eternal in human hearts no longer supported by temporal institutions which had seemed eternal but which were crashing on all sides."[24] That is essentially the work of love's mind also in our own times, very similar as it seems to those of the decline and fall of the Roman Empire. Now too love's mind has "to rekindle hearts in a world that grows chill," to bring to human consciousness the love that is at large in the universe and at work already in our hearts.

Our "deserted cities of the heart," the realms of life that have become unlived or uninhabited in our times, are especially those of love's mind, the realms of contemplation. Of the three lives, or dimensions of life, that Aristotle speaks of,[25] enjoyment and action and contemplation, the one that is largely missing for us is the contemplative life. We have the life of action and the life of enjoyment but that of contemplation leaves an empty place in our lives that tends to be filled by violence. A city of action and enjoyment without contemplation is a violent city. If I look for that realm in my own life, I have to discover it in the way I spend my time. When I give time to the spirit, when I practice "attention, the natural prayer of the soul," I feel a peace, I live in my own "center of stillness, surrounded by silence." When I give no time to the spirit, or go a while without giving any time to it, and spend all my time on action and enjoyment, on work and play, I feel rather a restlessness of the heart. And what is restlessness in me I can see is violence in the city. Still, this very restlessness is where contemplation begins,

> In the deserts of the heart
> Let the healing fountain start.[26]

Our restlessness is our way into rest. For us the realms of contemplation have become "places in the heart which do not yet exist," and our restlessness discovers them as places of repose, "and into them enters suffering that they may have existence." Our restlessness is our suffering, but we learn from suffering, we come to insight, when our restlessness becomes conscious as "negative love" that says "not this, not that." It is when we go on to make the positive print from the photographic negative, when we realize our restlessness is an experience of our soul's capacity for God, that we discover those "places in the heart." We can stop short, speaking simply of the "restlessness of desire," like Leo Bersani in *The Forms of Violence*, saying "the mobility of desire means that we are always moving away from the presumed objects of our desire,"[27] or we can go on with Augustine to say "our heart is restless until it rests in you," and then the very recollection of our life becomes an act of contemplation, like his *Confessions*, a remembering of love, a remembering of God, a search for God in time and memory.

It is by remembering love, by remembering God, by searching for God in time and memory, that I begin to know myself, to know my heart. I begin to understand the enthusiasms of my life, the many shapes of my heart's desire. "Were I to go where my heart dwells . . ." is a sentence that is not

easy to finish. It requires knowing my heart, knowing whether
it dwells in the realms of action or in those of enjoyment
or in those of contemplation. In our times the realms of
action and of enjoyment are close at hand. It is the realms
of contemplation that are far away, and it is those faraway
realms that are able to illumine the dark in which we live,
to be "a light for you in dark places," to be "a light when all
other lights go out." "Were I to go where my heart dwells . . ."
is a contrary-to-fact sentence, implying that I will not go there
but stay here. Still, it is the light from there that enables me
to live and to work here. It is the light of contemplation that
illumines action and enjoyment, or again, as the Quakers
say,[28] I have to bring the inner light to the world of action
and enjoyment and to bring the world to the inner light of
contemplation.

No doubt, to speak of a city of the heart is "poetry in
the dark ages," to speak of it as a city not only of action
and enjoyment but of contemplation. Nonetheless, the life
of contemplation is as real as the life of action and the life of
enjoyment. All the questions we have been asking have been
about the contemplative life: Do we love with a love we know
or with a love we do not know? What difference does love's
direction make? Do the voices that are heard in poetry tell
us of the essence of things? What does the heart's desire look
like in the mirror of death, in the magic of transfiguration,
and in the mystery of eternal life? Is the love of God simply
attention, the natural prayer of the soul? Is there a city of
the heart?

There is an answer to all these questions that is "no answer
in logic, but in excess of light."[29] It is the love Dante ends
with, "the love that moves the sun and the other stars," the
love the old man of the desert spoke of to T. E. Lawrence,
"The love is from God, and of God, and towards God."[30]
We meet the love most often, though, as "negative love," as
restless longing. I think of the melancholy you can sometimes
hear in Mozart's music. If I listen, I can hear the unrequited
longing of the heart,

Done in,
done with,
done for,
I live inside a tale
of letting be,
of openness to mystery,
and walk love's road
like no fool
like an old fool,
loving Holy Wisdom,
learning her eternal music,
getting rid of love I haven't got
to find the love I have
to love heart-free in time.

Two Song Cycles

Wisdom stands behind love's mind. I call her Ayasofya, using the Turkish name from the Greek name Hagia Sophia, as if it were a personal name for the figure of Holy Wisdom. I have been calling her that ever since visiting the Ayasofya in Istanbul ten years ago, but I wrote these hymns to Holy Wisdom only a year before starting on this book. I was thinking of Novalis and his *Hymns to the Night*. When I came to set the words to music, a melody I had thought of years before came to mind—it is the one given above in the chapter on "The Words and the Music." As soon as I thought of this one, others began to come, and when I began to write piano accompaniments I became very excited about the whole project, and what had started to be a cycle of only seven songs became a cycle of twenty-one, each group of seven ending with a song simply on the name Ayasofya, melismatic like an Alleluia.

"Songs about Songs," my second song cycle, was begun in the summer after finishing the chapter "The Friends of God" for this book. I call it "Songs about Songs" because music itself is a theme in the lyrics—it reflects my excitement about the way of music, the road not taken in my life, rejoining the way of words, the road taken. I had always accepted the idea of Robert Frost's poem "The Road Not Taken," that you had to give up forever all alternate lives in order to be heart and soul in your chosen life, but now I have the sense of an unexpected fullness of life that comes when the road you have given up rejoins the road you have chosen. It is like learning to love "with all your heart, and with all your soul, and with all your might."

---

*We recorded the first song cycle privately, with Kristen Sullivan singing soprano and me playing piano, and we had a little performance at Notre Dame in November of 1990 and at St. Albert's in Oakland in February of 1991.

Ayasofya
(Songs to Holy Wisdom)

I
Shadow of God

All hail, wisdom
of silence and the dark,
you are with God
and your bliss is with us
and we are blessed.
All holy wisdom,
shadow of God,
be with me,
always at work in me.

II
One

O Wisdom, lead me
from waking before you
to sleep in your surrounding,
and from finding rest
to dreaming of you and me,
and from dream to dreamless
sleep together,
and from one another
to one.

III
In the Lost Hills

I met you
dwelling in a human heart;
I found and lost you,
and I lost and found
my soul in the lost hills;
and we shall meet again

as child and child,
and heart shall speak peace
unto heart.
A human face
and your face in the azure light,
a human soul
and your soul of a universe,
and we shall meet again,
face to face,
and heart shall speak peace
unto heart.
To let friend befriend
and soul besoul,
to let be
and be heart-free
and heart-whole,
and we shall meet again
as friend and friend,
and heart shall speak peace
unto heart.

IV
Two Worlds

Now I live in two worlds:
I am young in one
and old in the other,
I am also outside
and telling of them;
so I live at once
in having
and not having
and in peace.

V
A Dream Dreaming of Us

There is a dream
dreaming of us,
a larger story

we awaken to
upon a mental voyage,
waking us to sleeping
when all things were once at one
and we could understand
the language of the sparrows.

VI

The World Is a Bridge

And now a moment with you
is enough to reassure me
all is well,
for this world is a bridge,
and we pass over it,
but do not build our house on it,
a rainbow bridge,
and we shall walk together
on and on into the light.
I feel behind me
there is sadness,
but before me
there is joy,
for one who is heart-free
has joy no one can take away,
and one who lets oneself
and lets God be
shall live in wandering joy,
and so shall we,
for we have chosen now
and let go of the road not taken
that was keeping us
from giving ourselves over
to the road that takes us
round and round
and ever on and on
into the light.

VII
Ayasofya

(no words but the name itself)

VIII
Repose in Light

On summer evenings
of childhood
I used to sit in twilight
and listen
to my grandfather telling
stories of longing
and of surprise.
I knew I too was in a story
and would someday meet the mystery
and ever after be its mirror,
for this is the magic
of an old man of the sea,
a woman of the earth,
a child of the fire
who knows the way of the rainbow,
to rekindle hearts
in a world that grows chill,
and to find repose in light.

IX
Nightmusic of the Soul

"Explore the realm of music,"
words I heard once in a dream,
may be the words unsaid in waking life
of far guidance,
of near assurance,
a lightning before death,
the inner light I seek,
and yet an utterance of command
I have not followed,
as it leads beyond all saying.

For when I choose my way
between the words and the music,
it is the words I choose,
as I dwell in them
and in the music I travel,
as when I sing
I am transposed into another world
where figure follows figure,
other and the same,
and feeling follows feeling
of movement and of rest
in places of the mind
that do not exist for me
until I go back in time
out of mind and call
to mind the dark
nightmusic of the soul.

X
Child's Way

My grandfather
would take me on a way
that later I would walk alone,
remembering a last
time I had passed a loved
red cedar and a mossyback along
the river running,
—I would stop and point
to see what he would call them,
and whatever he called anything,
that was its name.

XI
Soul's Way

My soul's way
passes along the seashore
where death is waiting
to make us young

by turning ends
into beginnings
in the waters,
and by showing us
the stairway winding
down into the heart of the earth
where life is watching
a crystal mirror
showing us what is not our self,
for earth is older than our death
and time is older than our earth,
and only plunging into the center
brings us to time
sitting and playing
as a child born in a kingdom
that is older still than time.

XII
Love Is Round

Where do you come from
and where are you going?
we ask one another
when we meet again.
The world is round, we answer,
but the road goes ever on and on.
And what do you desire?
we ask each other.
God is my desire, we say,
for love is round,
is from and of and toward,
and love goes ever on and on.

XIII
You in You

I look into your infinite eyes
and see the tiny image
that is me,
and I long to see you in you

and not only me,
for when the knower is known
and the lover is loved,
then you are and I am,
and you and I are one.

XIV
Ayasofya

(no words but the name itself)

XV
Long Desire

A long desire
comes back to me,
a longing desiring
to have,
to be a friend,
even a lover of God,
the lofty ambition
of loving—
the heart's desire
to be oned,
ascending
from passion
to ecstasy
in contemplation
of all.

XVI
Universal Word

My ears open to silence
and my eyes to the dark,
to learn my own true name
and all names nameless under the sun,
of underground streams,
of unborn children,
the unvoiced consonants

of a universal word
breathed by the rising
and the setting of the stars,
a word become flesh
among us,
coming and going
as a breath of human life.

XVII
Unsung Song

Words without music
can seem empty,
and music without words
can seem blind,
but I listen now
for the unsung song of words
and for the unspoken speech of music,
for we know more
than we can say,
and we say nothing
without relying
on what we cannot say
of the silence between words,
of the dark between lights,
of the dying between lives,
the higher emptiness,
the unnameable delight.

XVIII
The Dream Is Timeless

Is silence our untold story?
Is the dark our unshining light?
Is death our unlived life?
There is time to tell
of things I remember
and things I dream,
but the dream is timeless,

and things are meant,
and there are signs,
and the heart speaks,
and there is a way.

XIX
Earth Balancing

I can feel you
in earth balancing
and in nightshining sky,
in watchful spirits
and in words of flesh.
Is it you I want
in wanting?
Is it you I fear
in fearing?
—The mystery draws me on,
I feel the serenity
and the adventure of it,
and I know it is my way,
though it goes past the view
of every story I can tell,
shows itself in words
and then withdraws.
I can only let be
and be open to its showing,
waiting on words unsaid.

XX
Light & Shadow, Walls & Space

Walls
shut out your light,
and yet your shadow
fills the space,
and you are here
with us,
our shadows
cast by presence,

and we are longing
for the presence
in the shadow dance
beyond the shadow cone,
the umbra of the moon,
for there walls
open onto space,
and shadows
dance with light.

XXI
Ayasofya

(no words but the name itself)

Songs about Songs

I
Longview

By the longview
of the universe of night
I know I do not know
my coming and my going,
and I call on you,
the soul of wisdom,
be my muse in music,
guiding me and guarding me
in life in light in love.

II
*My Blind Master**

Once the way of music
was my way,

---

*In memory of Carl Mathes (1896–1957)

and my blind master wished
to teach me how to listen
as the blind do
and to improvise,
but now the way of words
has been my way
into the dark with love,
and now I listen like the blind,
and hearing,
I compose.

III
Life after Life

Give me time, my God,
to round the cycle of my songs,
so that more willingly I can
let go of everything I love,
and yet my heart will live
within me, I believe,
and will not perish in my dying,
though some songs are still unsung,
and powers still unused,
and needs and longings unrequited,
—it must be
for life to be life after life.

IV
Inside a Song

Why begin? Why end?
Why not go on and on?
Life is a timeless festival,
and we who improvise are playing,
and the music is a state of being
and not just symbolic form,
but we who sing and listen come and go,
and my song does begin and end,
attention is my prayer of soul,
and here is my beginning and my ending,

where I am,
inside a song.

V
*Unchanging Number**

Tell me, Master,
how you turn
from changing to unchanging number
and are sensible to
music of eternal life,
or tell me rather how to listen
to unchanging number in the changing
and to hear eternal music
in the song of earth.

VI
My Other and My Same

My heart is holy
if I love,
but I rely on being loved
—my same is other
and my other is my same,
myself in rhythmic being
and in singing movement
and in breathing rest
in you, more truly me than I.

VII
Earth's Shadow Rising

Are you waiting
in the dark and deepening of life?
—I look there into changing light,
remembering the love

---

*To Saint Augustine on reading his *De Musica*

I knew in this same gold, this red,
this purple at life's dawning
—in the afterglow I see
earth's shadow rising,
and the right ascension
and the declination of the stars
—I listen to their joy
and hear the song of my return.

VIII
Along the Solar Walk

I knew the wonder as I lay
and looked up into summer night,
it is and I am,
and I knew my separation,
I am here
and not there,
I knew my loneliness, I am
a way a lone a last a loved
along the solar walk,
a way of friends,
a song of ascents
you have given me.

IX
The Real of Desire

I am someone
no one else is,
and I am something
everyone is
—so I love and sing
what no one knows,
and yet desire to be known
to be understood
—Is that the real of my desire
that I meet only in my dreams?
Or is it you I meet,
unknowing the unknown?

X
The Unvoiced Word

Wisdom's spirit
comes to me in happy ending tales
that shape the project of my life,
in sayings of a providence
I weave into a peaceful vision,
and in universal songs
I make into my music
and in endless dances
I dance in free rhythm,
as I learn to sing and listen
to the unvoiced
word of life.

XI
Eternal Not Immortal

Your song is eternal
not immortal
like the laughter,
irrepressible,
of gods at human folly
and our fate
that could not reach them
as it reaches you,
the Lord with us,
our companion
on our journey
home to you.

XII
That Individual

A long night's worry
over words
that are discouraging
—will my heartburning
stop when evening

comes again and calm?
Or does my heart desire too much?
No,—the peace that comes
is full and by
and unresigned
—I am that individual,
I have something to sing.

XIII
*Near and Far**

You are near
and far,
if where danger is
there is salvation
—give us keenness
like the flying eyes
that gaze into the chasm,
for the high horizons of our time
surround us as our day is ending,
and we hear the crickets
and the river and the song
of unfulfilled desire.

XIV
Music in Memory

We are so many
on the earth
we fear
we are of no account,
lives leaping up
and thriving
and then falling
and then withering
—so let us turn to love
that turns to music in our memory

----

*A prayer on reading Hölderlin

—it sings to God, and I will sing
and will make music to the Only One.

XV
Ebb and Flood

God ebbs
and floods in memory,
and love encloses
all I sing
and what is lasting
of enthusiasm,
minding
and reminding me
of once and wonder
of illumining and now
of kindling once
again to love.

Notes

A Late Summer Night's Dream

1. See my article "St. Thomas' Theology of Participation" in *Theological Studies* 18 (1957): 487ff.

2. *A Midsummer Night's Dream*, act 1, scene 1, lines 232–239 in *Sixteen Plays of Shakespeare*, ed. by George Lyman Kittredge (Boston: Ginn, 1946), p. 154.

3. Sylvia Shaw Judson, *The Quiet Eye*: "A Way of Looking at Pictures" (Washington, D.C.: Regnery, 1982).

4. *As You Like It*, act 2, scene 7, lines 139–140 in Kittredge, *op.cit.*, p. 283. Kittredge gives the exchange of verses in his introduction to the play, p. 269.

5. Psalm 46:10 (Revised Standard Version).

6. T. E. Lawrence, *Seven Pillars of Wisdom* (Harmondsworth, England: Penguin and Jonathan Cape, 1971), p. 364. See my *Reasons of the Heart* (New York: Macmillan, 1978; rpt. Notre Dame, Ind.: University of Notre Dame Press, 1979), p. 1.

7. Aquinas, *De veritate*, q.1, a.2. See my discussion in *The Church of the Poor Devil* (New York: Macmillan, 1982; rpt. Notre Dame: University of Notre Dame Press, 1983), p. 135.

8. See Roland Barthes, *A Lover's Discourse*, trans. Richard Howard (New York: Hill & Wang, 1978) and see my discussion in *The House of Wisdom* (San Francisco: Harper & Row, 1985; rpt. Notre Dame: University of Notre Dame Press, 1993), pp. 96–104.

9. *A Midsummer Night's Dream*, act 4, scene 1, lines 194–195 in Kittredge, *op.cit.*, p. 170.

10. Martin Heidegger, *Discourse on Thinking*, a translation of *Gelassenheit* by John M. Anderson and E. Hans Freund (New York: Harper & Row, 1969), p. 55. See my discussion in *Peace of the Present* (Notre Dame: University of Notre Dame Press, 1991), pp. 10–18.

11. Julia Kristeva, *In the Beginning Was Love*: "Psychoanalysis and Faith," trans. Arthur Goldhammer (New York: Columbia University Press, 1987), p. 23.

12. Barbara C. Anderson, "Kierkegaard's Despair as a Religious Author," *International Journal for Philosophy of Religion* 4 (Winter 1973): 243.

141

13. Patricia McKillip, *The Moon and the Face* (New York: Berkley, 1986), p. 88.

14. On "the eyes of faith" in Aquinas' vision see Pierre Rousselot, *The Eyes of Faith*, trans. Joseph Donceel (New York: Fordham, 1990).

15. Heraclitus, fragment 18 (my translation) in Hermann Diels, *Fragmente der Vorsokratiker*, 5th ed., vol. 1 (Berlin: Weidmann, 1934), p. 155. See my discussion in *Reasons of the Heart*, p. 92.

16. A phrase from Saint John of the Cross. See my discussion in *The House of Wisdom*, p. 6.

The Friends of God

1. John Henry Newman, *An Essay on the Development of Christian Doctrine*, ed. by J. M. Cameron (Baltimore: Penguin, 1974), p. 114. He is quoting here from one of his own University Sermons.

2. See my discussion of these sayings about "heart to heart" in *The House of Wisdom*, p. 6 (Newman) and 10 (Beethoven).

3. Newman, *A Grammar of Assent* (Notre Dame and London: University of Notre Dame Press, 1979), p. 276. See my discussion of this passage in *The Homing Spirit* (New York: Crossroad, 1987), p. 2.

4. J. R. R. Tolkien, *The Lord of the Rings* (London: Allen & Unwin, 1969), p. 903.

5. Luke 2:35 (King James Version).

6. Tolkien, *Smith of Wooton Major* (Boston: Houghton Mifflin, 1967), p. 36.

7. Walter Benjamin, "The Storyteller" in his *Illuminations* ed. by Hannah Arendt and trans. by Harry Zohn (New York: Schocken, 1969), p. 83.

8. Ibid., p. 86.

9. Simone Weil, *Waiting for God*, trans. by Emma Craufurd (New York: Putnam, 1951), p. 135. See my discussion in *The Peace of the Present*, pp. 61, 68–69.

10. Henry Chadwick in his introduction to his translation of Saint Augustine, *Confessions* (Oxford: Oxford University Press, 1991), p. xxiv. On the four cycles of story see my *Peace of the Present*, pp. 71–72. On time's arrow becoming love's direction see my *House of Wisdom*, pp. 103–104.

11. Benjamin, "The Storyteller," p. 87.

12. See *The Spiritual Exercises of St. Ignatius Loyola*, trans. by Thomas Corbishley (Wheathampstead, Hertfordshire: Anthony Clarke, 1973), pp. 107–114. I am interpreting the transition from the first week (pp. 107–111) to the second (pp. 111–114) as a passing from outer to inner influences.

13. See my discussion of this saying of Hammarskjöld's in my *Peace of the Present*, p. 93.

14. Benjamin, "The Storyteller," p. 90.

15. Ibid., p. 93. Plato's definition is in *Timaeus* 37d (my translation).

16. Meister Eckhart quoted by Martin Heidegger in his essay "The Thing" in *Poetry, Language, Thought*, trans. by Alfred Hofstadter (New York: Harper & Row, 1975), p. 176.

17. Patricia McKillip, *The Sorceress and the Cygnet* (New York: Ace, 1991), p. 92.

18. I take this phrase from the prologue to *Dark Night of the Soul* by Saint John of the Cross, trans. by E. Allison Peers (New York: Doubleday, 1990), p. 34.

19. Tolkien, *The Lord of the Rings*, p. 87.

20. Benjamin, "The Storyteller," p. 91.

21. Kenneth White, *The Blue Road* (Edinburgh: Mainstream, 1990), p. 11. On time turning into space see what he says about "a move from history to geography," p. 64. On things in their nakedness and wind blowing anonymously see his concluding poem, pp. 154–160.

22. Tolkien, *The Lord of the Rings*, p. 292.

23. Newman, *Prose and Poetry*, ed. by George N. Shuster (New York: Allyn & Bacon, 1925), p. 116.

24. Marcel Proust, *Remembrance of Things Past*, trans. by C. Scott Moncrieff, T. Kilmartin, and A. Mayor (New York: Random House, 1981), vol. 3, p. 906.

25. Benjamin, "The Storyteller," pp. 86–87.

26. Tolkien, *The Lord of the Rings*, p. 540.

27. Dante, *Paradiso* 3:85, in *Dante's Paradiso*, trans. by P. H. Wicksteed (London: J. M. Dent, 1958), p. 31. See my discussion in *The Homing Spirit*, p. 9. The phrase "a way of avoiding the real of desire" is Jacques Lacan's in Slavoj Zizek, *Looking Awry* (Camridge, Mass. and London: MIT Press, 1991), p. 48.

28. Leon Bloy, *Pilgrim of the Absolute*, selections by Raïssa Martain, trans. John Coleman and Harry Lorin Binsse (New York: Pantheon, 1947), p. 349. See my discussion in *The Peace of The Present*, p. 103.

29. Tolkien, *The Lord of the Rings*, p. 518.

30. Joseph Conrad, *Heart of Darkness* (New York: Penguin, 1978), p. 89. See my discussion in *The Church of the Poor Devil*, p. 13.

31. Dag Hammarskjöld, *Markings*, trans. by Leif Sjöberg and W. H. Auden (New York: Ballantine, 1985), p. 138.

32. Benjamin, "The Storyteller," p. 94.

33. John 9:4 (King James Version).

34. Novalis quoted by George MacDonald, *Phantastes and Lilith*, with intro. by C. S. Lewis (London: Victor Gollancz, 1962), p. 180 and p. 420.

35. Albert Camus, *Notebooks 1942–1951*, trans. by Justin O'Brien (New York: Knopf, 1965), p. 55. See Søren Kierkegaard, *Purity of Heart Is to Will One Thing*, trans. by Douglas V. Steere (New York: Harper, 1948).

36. MacDonald, *Phantastes and Lilith*, p. 114 (chap. 15 of *Phantastes*).

37. Ibid., p. 62 (chap. 8 of *Phantastes*).

38. Saint John of the Cross, *Dark Night of the Soul*, p. 89.

39. Genesis 1:2 (RSV). See my discussion in *The Church of the Poor Devil*, p. 46.

40. Hammarskjöld, *Markings*, p. 69.

41. W. J. Turner, *Mozart* (San Francisco: Heron House, 1989), pp. 26–27. This essay of Turner's appeared in Hubert J. Foss, ed., *The Heritage of Music*, vol. 1 (Oxford: Oxford University Press, 1927). Although I am quoting from Turner's perceptive essay here, I do not mean to agree with

his conclusion, "Mozart could not make that affirmation" (p. 27). On the contrary, see what I say a few paragraphs further on, about Mozart singing of the hour of death.

42. Hammarskjöld, *Markings*, p. 81.

43. Newman, *A Grammar of Assent*, p. 276 (cited above in note 3). He is quoting from Sirach, that is, Ecclesiasticus 4:19–20 (Douay Version).

44. Wisdom of Solomon (= Wisdom in the Douay Version) 8:2.

45. Benjamin, "The Storyteller," p. 99.

46. Kierkegaard, *Philosophical Fragments*, trans. by David F. Swenson and Howard V. Hong (Princeton: Princeton University Press, 1962), p. 53.

47. See her *Life*, trans. by E. Allison Peers, *The Complete Works of Saint Teresa of Jesus*, vol. 1 (New York: Sheed & Ward, 1946), pp. 109–111. See my discussion in *The Way of All the Earth* (New York: Macmillan, 1972; rpt. Notre Dame: University of Notre Dame Press, 1978), pp. 116–117.

48. Turner, *Mozart*, p. 25.

The Words and the Music

1. Marcel Proust, *On Reading*, bilingual text trans. and ed. by Jean Autret and William Burford (New York: Macmillan, 1971), p. 35.

2. Saint Thomas Aquinas, *De Ente et Essentia* ad finem in *Opuscula Omnia*, ed. by Joannes Perrier (Paris: P. Lethielleux, 1949), vol. 1, p. 50 (my translation).

3. See my discussion of "Nothing, Lord, but you" in *The House of Wisdom*, p. 16.

4. *The Cloud of Unknowing and Other Works*, trans. by Clifton Wolters (London: Penguin, 1978), p. 211 (from the Middle English trans. of *The Mystical Theology* of Dionysius the Areopagite).

5. T. S. Eliot, *The Three Voices of Poetry* (New York: Cambridge University Press, 1954), p. 33.

6. *Troilus and Cressida*, act 4, scene 5, line 60, and *Richard II*, act 5, scene 5, line 9.

7. Eliot, *The Three Voices of Poetry*, p. 5.

8. Proust, *On Reading*, p. 67 (the French on facing p. 66). Here he is speaking of architecture, but he means it to apply to books.

9. Ibid., p. 3.

10. Loren Eiseley reports hearing this said by a philosopher in *The Night Country* (New York: Scribner, 1971), p. 166.

11. Tolkien, "On Fairy-Stories" in *The Tolkien Reader* (New York: Ballantine, 1978), p. 41.

12. T. S. Eliot quoting Juliana of Norwich in *Four Quartets* (New York: Harcourt Brace Jovanovich, 1971), pp. 56, 57, and 59 ("Little Gidding," lines 167–168, 196–197, and 255–256).

13. Erik Erikson, *The Life Cycle Completed* (New York: Norton, 1985), p. 62.

14. Beethoven, Opus 135 (String Quartet in F major). I am using the Philharmonia edition (Vienna: Wiener Philharmonischer Verlag, 1936), p. 20.

15. See Milan Kundera's discussion of these words in his novel *The Unbearable Lightness of Being*, trans. by Michael Henry Heim (New York: Harper Perennial, 1991), pp. 32–35 and p. 195.

16. Proust, *On Reading*, p. 15 and p. 19.

17. Ibid., p. 31.

18. See Werner Heisenberg, "Remarks on the Origin of the Relations of Uncertainty" in William C. Price and Seymour S. Chissick, eds., *Uncertainty Principle and Foundations of Quantum Mechanics* (New York: Wiley, 1977), pp. 3–6.

19. Max Brod, *Franz Kafka*, trans. by G. Humphreys Roberts and Richard Winston (New York: Schocken, 1964), p. 196. See my discussion in *Reasons of the Heart*, p. 5.

20. Brod, ibid.

21. On *lectio divina* see chap. 48 of *The Rule of St. Benedict*, ed. in Latin and English by Timothy Fry (Collegeville, Minn.: Liturgical Press, 1981), pp. 248–253. See the discussion by Jean Leclercq, *The Love of Learning and the Desire for God* (New York: Fordham, 1982), pp. 15 and 72.

22. Psalm 33:11 (RSV).

23. Proust, *On Reading*, p. 31.

24. Ibid., p. 65.

25. Isaiah 55:8 (RSV).

26. John 1:14 and 6:68 (RSV).

27. John 1:18 and 13:23 (cf. also 13:25 and 21:20) (RSV).

28. Martin Buber, *Good and Evil*, trans. by Ronald Gregor Smith and Michael Bullock (New York: Scribner, 1953), p. 43. See my discussion in *The Homing Spirit*, p. 65.

29. Jacques Derrida, *Positions*, trans. by Alan Bass (Chicago: University of Chicago Press, 1982), p. 14.

30. W. J. Turner, *Mozart*, pp. 15–16.

31. A saying of Malebranche quoted by Walter Benjamin and Paul Celan. See my discussion in *Peace of the Present*, pp. 86 and 104. See Paul Celan, *Collected Prose*, trans. by Rosemarie Waldrop (Riverdale-on-Hudson, NY: Sheep Meadow, 1986), p. 50, and see Walter Benjamin, *Illuminations*, p. 1?

32. This passage is quoted by Peter Kivy, *Music Alone* (Ithaca and London: Cornell, 1990), p. vi, who uses it to structure his whole book on pure music. I add Forster's conclusion "in any case, the passion of your life becomes more vivid" from the same page of the novel: E. M. Forster, *Howards End* (New York: Random-Vintage, 1989), p. 32 (opening of chap. 5).

33. Saint Augustine, *Confessions*, trans. by Henry Chadwick (Oxford: Oxford University Press, 1991), p. 164 and pp. 207–208.

34. Lines from Paul Claudel, *The Tidings Brought to Mary*, act 4, scene 2. See my discussion in *Peace of the Present*, pp. 43–44.

35. Herbert Read, *The Green Child* (New York: New Directions, 1948), p. 12. See my discussion in *The House of Wisdom*, p. 3.

36. Charles O. Hartman, *Jazz Text* (Princeton: Princeton University Press, 1991), p. 9.

37. Celan, *Collected Prose*, p. 50.

38. Mozart quoted by Jacques Hadamard, *The Psychology of Invention in the Mathematical Field* (Princeton: Princeton University Press, 1945), p. 16.

39. W. B. Yeats, *A Vision* (New York: Collier, 1966), p. 220. See my discussion in *Time and Myth* (New York: Doubleday, 1973; rpt. Notre Dame: University of Notre Dame Press, 1975), p. 5.

40. Willard Ropes Trask, *The Unwritten Song*, vol. 1 (New York: Macmillan, 1966), p. 80. See my discussion in *Reasons of the Heart*, p. 2.

41. See my discussion of Ayasofya in *The House of Wisdom*, p. ix and pp. 25–54.

42. I am using the "new revision": Igor Stravinsky, *Symphony of Psalms* (London: Boosey & Hawkes, 1948). The psalms are Psalm 38: 13 and 14, Psalm 39:2–4, and Psalm 150 in the Latin Vulgate. English translations here are mine.

43. 2 Samuel 6:14 (RSV).

44. Kafka, *The Great Wall of China*, trans. by Willa and Edwin Muir (New York: Schocken, 1946), p. 306 (Aphorism #101). I have "one's fellow human beings" for "his fellow men."

45. Turner, *Mozart*, p. 25.

46. J. G. Arapura, *Religion as Anxiety and Tranquillity* (The Hague and Paris: Mouton, 1972).

47. Eliot, *The Three Voices of Poetry*, p. 35.

48. Kierkegaard, *The Concept of Dread*, trans. by Walter Lowrie (Princeton: Princeton University Press, 1957), p. 139.

49. Heidegger, *Discourse on Thinking*, p. 55 (cited above in "A Late Summer Night's Dream," note 10). But see Heidegger's rejection of an approach to time through eternity at the beginning of his early work *The Concept of Time*, trans. by William McNeill (Oxford: Blackwell, 1992), p. 1.

50. Simone Weil, *The Need for Roots*, trans. by Arthur Wills (New York: Putnam, 1952), pp. 187 and 188.

Three Movements of Contemplation

1. These questions are the opening words of Lawrence Thornton's novel *Under the Gypsy Moon* (New York: Doubleday, 1990), p. 3.

2. Tolkien, *The Lord of the Rings*, p. 399.

3. Saint Thomas Aquinas, *Summa Theologiae*, II-II, question 180, article 6. I am using the edition of The Medieval Institute of Ottawa, 1942, vol. 3, pp. 2312–2314 (my own translation here).

4. Rainer Maria Rilke, *Stories of God*, trans. by M. D. Herter Norton (New York: Norton, 1963), p. 29.

5. Saint Augustine, *Confessions*, trans. by Henry Chadwick, p. 3.

6. Artur Lundkvist, *Journeys in Dream and Imagination*, trans. by Ann B. Weissmann and Annika Plank (New York: 4 Walls 8 Windows, 1991), p. 23.

7. Ibid., p. 129.

8. Henri Nouwen, *Beyond the Mirror* (New York: Crossroad, 1990).

9. Tolkien, "On Fairy-Stories" in *The Tolkien Reader* (New York: Ballantine, 1978), p. 52.

10. Heinrich Böll, *The Clown*, trans. by Leila Vennewitz (New York: Avon, 1975), p. 131.

11. See my discussion in *The Homing Spirit*, p. 46, but there I take the three movements of contemplation in a different way, "the linear from image to image, the oblique from image to insight, and the circular around insight."

12. Marcel Marceau, *Pimporello*, adapted and ed. by Robert Hammond (London: Peter Owen, 1991), p. 88 (ending) and p. 5 (beginning).

13. See my discussion of three sentences from *Don Quixote* in *The Homing Spirit*, pp. 98–99.

14. Marceau, *Pimporello*, p. 7.

15. Ibid., p. 88.

16. Michael Polanyi, *The Tacit Dimension* (Gloucester, Mass.: Peter Smith, 1983), p. 4. See my discussion in *Time and Myth*, pp. 109–117.

17. John 17:9 (RSV).

18. Marceau, *Pimporello*, p. 88.

19. Francis Bacon, *Memorial of Access* in *The Works of Francis Bacon*, ed. by James Spedding, Robert Leslie Ellis, and Douglas Denon Heath (London: Longmans, 1874), vol. 14, p. 351. The *Memorial of Access* is something Bacon wrote after his impeachment and fall as Lord Chancellor. It is a memo for an interview with the king discussing his situation after his fall, outlining the writing projects he wants to undertake.

20. Heidegger, *The Concept of Time*, p. 22 (conclusion).

21. George MacDonald, *Phantastes and Lilith*, p. 182 (the ending of *Phantastes*).

22. Polanyi, *The Tacit Dimension*, pp. 13–19.

23. My translation of *Noverim me, noverim te* in Augustine's *Soliloquies* (Augustine's opening prayer in Book 2). See my discussion in *A Search for God in Time and Memory* (New York: Macmillan, 1969; rpt. Notre Dame: University of Notre Dame Press, 1977), p. 51.

24. Tolstoy as quoted by Max Gorky, *Reminiscences of Tolstoy, Chekhov, and Andreev*, trans. by Katherine Mansfield, S. S. Koteliansky, and Leonard Woolf (London: Hogarth, 1948), p. 23.

25. Paul Valery, *Introduction to the Method of Leonardo da Vinci*, trans. by Thomas McGreevy (London: John Rodker, 1929), especially pp. 9 and 32.

26. Polanyi, *The Tacit Dimension*, p. 10 ("attending from" and "attending to"), p. 18 (destructive scrutiny), and p. 19 (reintegration).

27. Shakespeare, *I Henry IV*, act 2, scene 4, lines 358–359 in *The Pelican Shakespeare*, ed. by Alfred Harbage (Baltimore: Penguin, 1969), p. 685.

28. B. F. Skinner, *Particulars of My Life* (New York: Knopf, 1976). The sequel was *The Shaping of a Behaviorist* (New York: Knopf, 1979).

29. Tolkien, *The Lord of the Rings*, p. 439.

30. Heidegger, *Being and Time*, trans. by John Macquarrie and Edward Robinson (New York: Harper & Row, 1962), p. 19.

31. Newman's motto, *cor ad cor loquitur*. See my discussion in *House of Wisdom*, p. 6.

32. *Franz Schubert's Letters and Other Writings*, ed. by O. E. Deutsch, trans. by Venetia Saville (London: Faber & Gwyer, 1928), p. 60.

33. Ibid., p. 61 and p. 59 (titles and footnote).

34. C. S. Lewis, *Surprised by Joy* (London: Geoffrey Bles, 1955), pp. 23–24. See my discussion in *Church of the Poor Devil*, p. 98.

35. M. L. Haskins quoted by King George VI in a Christmas broadcast in 1939, *King George VI to His Peoples* (London: John Murray, 1952), p. 21.

36. Heidegger, *The Concept of Time*, p. 11.

37. *Franz Schubert's Letters*, p. 61.

38. Martin Buber, *I and Thou*, trans. by Ronald Gregor Smith (New York: Scribner's, 1958), p. 63.

39. Austin Tappan Wright, *Islandia* (New York: Farrar & Rinehart, 1942), pp. 372–374, 377, 639, and 971.

40. *The Road Goes Ever On*, music by Donald Swann, words by J. R. R. Tolkien (Boston: Houghton Mifflin, 1967).

41. I am using the score in Franz Schubert, *Complete Song Cycles*, ed. by Eusebius Mandyczewski (New York: Dover, 1970). Cf. Susan Youens, *Retracing a Winter's Journey: Schubert's Winterreise* (Ithaca & London: Cornell University Press, 1991).

42. T. S. Eliot, *Four Quartets*, p. 32 (at the end of "East Coker").

43. Mary Stewart, *Merlin Trilogy* (New York: William Morrow, 1980), pp. 52 and 57.

44. Theodore Adorno, *Alban Berg* (Cambridge: Cambridge University Press, 1991), p. 10 (speaking of the last days of Berg and those of Schubert).

45. Richard Strauss, *Vier Letze Lieder (Four Last Songs)*, vocal score, trans. by Michael Hamburger (New York: Boosey & Hawkes, 1959), p. 28.

46. Tolkien, *The Lord of the Rings*, p. 730. I am using the scores by Arnold Schoenberg of *Verklärte Nacht* (Opus 4, Vienna: Universal Edition, 1917 and 1943) and *Pierrot Lunaire* (Opus 21, Vienna: Universal Edition, 1914 and 1941).

47. Pindar, *Pythian*, iii, as quoted by Albert Camus in the epigaph to *The Myth of Sisyphus*, trans. by Justin O'Brien (New York: Knopf, 1961), p. 2.

48. Thomas Mann, *Doctor Faustus*, trans. by H. T. Lowe-Porter (New York: Vintage, 1992), p. 249.

49. Roland Barthes, *A Lover's Discourse*, trans. by Richard Howard (New York: Hill & Wang, 1978), p. 151.

50. Hermann Broch, *The Death of Virgil*, trans. by Jean Starr Untermeyer (San Francisco: North Point, 1983), pp. 17 (heart of light), 18 (longing fear), and 19 (heart's desire).

51. I am quoting all through this paragraph from W. B. Yeats, *A Vision* (New York: Collier, 1971), pp. 140–145 (his Phase 17).

52. See my discussion of this saying in *The Church of the Poor Devil*, p. 80.

53. Shakespeare, *The Tempest*, act 1, scene 2, lines 49–50 (p. 1374 in *The Pelican Shakespeare*).

54. See James Hamilton-Peterson's novel on this late adventure in Elgar's life, *Gerontius* (New York: Soho, 1991).

55. Jorge Luis Borges, "The Meeting in a Dream" in his *Other Inquisitions*, trans. by Ruth L. C. Simms (New York: Washington Square, 1966), pp. 101ff. Dante uses the phrase *alta fantasia* to describe what he is doing in the *Divine Comedy* in the very last canto, *Paradiso*, canto 33, line 142. The saying "all real living is meeting" is from Martin Buber, *I and Thou*, p. 11.

56. Broch, *The Death of Virgil*, p. 20.

57. Helen Luke, "Choice in the Lord of the Rings," an unpublished essay of hers that I quoted also in *The Peace of the Present*, p. 22.

58. Max Jacob in his preface to *The Dice Cup*, his book of prose poems ed. by Michael Brownstein (New York: SUNY, 1979), p. 7. See my discussion in *The House of Wisdom*, p. 111.

59. *Franz Schubert's Letters*, p. 61. This reminds me of Novalis and his *Hymns to the Night*.

60. Ibid.

61. Matthew 26: 39 and 42 (RSV).

62. Helen Waddell, *Poetry in the Dark Ages* (New York: Barnes & Noble, 1960), p. 1.

63. Broch, *The Death of Virgil*, p. 131. "What's a saint?" is from Newman, *The Dream of Gerontius* (London: Longmans, Green, 1904), line 453 (p. 45) and Elgar's music, *The Dream of Gerontius* (London: Novello, 1928), p. 84. The phrase "to do the right deed for the wrong reason" is from T. S. Eliot, *Murder in the Cathedral* (New York: Harcourt, Brace, 1935), p. 44.

64. Waddell, *Poetry in the Dark Ages*, p. 18.

65. Ibid., p. 22–23.

66. Ibid., p. 26.

67. Broch, *The Death of Virgil*, p. 482.

68. I am using the score by George Crumb, *Ancient Voices of Children* (New York: C. F. Peters, 1970), and his remarks on the inside cover. The words of the songs are from Federico Garcia Lorca, *Selected Poems* (New York: New Directions, 1955).

The Lovers of God

1. The full title of *The Cloud of Unknowing* was "a book of contemplation, the which is called The Cloud of Unknowing, in the which a soul is oned with God," *The Cloud of Unknowing and Other Works*, ed. by Clifton Wolters (New York: Penguin, 1978), p. 46.

2. A. S. Byatt, *Possession* (New York: Random House, 1990). The jacket painting, "The Beguiling of Merlin," is by Sir Edward Burne-Jones.

3. See Meister Eckhart quoted above in "The Friends of God," note 16.

4. Saint Augustine, *Confessions*, Book 10, chap. 27 (Chadwick, p. 201).

5. Tolkien, *The Lord of the Rings*, p. 516.

6. Ibid., p. 848.

7. F. Scott Fitzgerald, *Crack-Up* (New York: New Directions, 1945), p. 80.

8. "Where then did I find you to be able to learn of you? You were not already in my memory before I learnt of you. Where then did I find you so that I could learn of you if not in the fact that you transcend me?" Saint Augustine, *Confessions*, Book 10, chap. 26 (Chadwick, p. 201).

9. My translation of the sentence "Diligere autem Deum super omnia est quiddam connaturale homini" in Aquinas, *Summa Theologiae*, vol. 2 (I-II, question 109, article 3) (Ottawa: Medieval Institute of Ottawa, 1941), p. 1354B.

10. Nicolas Malebranche, *Oeuvres*, ed. by Genevieve Rodis-Lewis and Germain Malbreil (Paris: Gallimard, 1979), vol. 1, p. 1132. The saying is discussed by Walter Benjamin, *Illumination*, p. 134, and Paul Celan, *Collected Prose*, p. 50.

11. My translation of "L'attention de l'esprit est la prière naturelle que nous faisons à la vérité intérieur, afin qu'elle se découvre à nous" (Malebranche, *op. cit.*, p. 1132).

12. My translation of "Mais cette souveraine vérité ne repond pas toujours à nos désirs, parce que nous ne savons pas trop bien comment il la faut prier" (ibid.).

13. I Samuel 3:4, 6, 9, and 10 (Revised Standard Version).

14. My translation of the song,

> Muérome de amores,
> carillo, qué hare?
> —Que te mueras, alahé!

quoted by Willis Barnstone in his introduction to *The Poems of St. John of the Cross* (New York: New Directions, 1972), p. 13.

15. Proust, *On Reading*, p. 17 (I have slightly modified the translation, using the French on the facing page, inserting the word "only" and changing "non-ego" to "not me").

16. My translation of the opening verses of the poem "Entréme donde no supe" in San Juan de la Cruz, *Poesías Completas*, ed. by Cristobal Cuevas (Barcelona: Ediciones B, 1988), p. 102.

17. Kant, *The Critique of Pure Reason*. See my discussion of Kant's three questions in my *City of the Gods* (New York: Macmillan, 1965; rpt. Notre Dame: University of Notre Dame Press, 1978), p. 217.

18. Dylan Thomas, *Collected Poems* (New York: New Directions, 1957), p. 128.

19. Tolkien, *The Lord of the Rings*, p. 953.

20. Ibid., p. 973.

21. C. G. Jung, *Answer to Job*, trans. by R. F. C. Hull (New York: Meridian, 1960), p. 184. See my discussion in *The Way of All the Earth*, p. 189.

22. Marcus Aurelius, *Meditations*, trans. by Maxwell Staniforth (Baltimore: Penguin, 1964), p. 35.

23. The Merle sings "A lusty lyfe in luves service bene" and the Nightingale sings "All love is lost bot upone God allone," *Selections from*

the Poems of William Dunbar, ed. by Hugh MacDiarmid (Edinburgh: Oliver & Boyd, 1952), pp. 13–16.

24. William Wordsworth, "Preface to Lyrical Ballads" in *William Wordsworth*, ed. by Stephen Gill (Oxford and New York: Oxford University Press, 1990), p. 611.

25. John 18:9 (RSV).

26. Proust, *On Reading*, pp. 39 ("incapable of willing") and 41 ("an intervention").

27. Here I am translating the phrase "auxilio gratiae naturam sanantis" in Aquinas, *Summa Theologiae*, vol. 2 (I–II, question 109, article 3), p. 1355a.

28. Georg Trakl as quoted by Kenneth White in *The Blue Road*, p. 6. See Heidegger's interpretation of the "blue soul" and the "dark road" in his essay on Trakl's poetry in *On the Way to Language*, trans. by Peter D. Hertz (San Francisco: Harper San Francisco, 1982), pp. 159–198, especially his commentary on the line, "Soon blue soul and long journey," pp. 170–172.

29. Roland Barthes, *A Lover's Discourse*, p. 1. See my discussion in *The House of Wisdom*, pp. 96 and 100–101.

30. Heidegger as quoted by Kenneth White in *The Blue Road*, p. 7. Peter Hertz has a more literal translation in Heidegger, *On the Way to Language*, p. 163.

31. Ron Paquin and Robert Doherty, *Not First in Nobody's Heart* (Ames, Iowa: Iowa State University Press, 1992), p. 260.

32. *George MacDonald: An Anthology*, ed. by C. S. Lewis (New York: Macmillan, 1978), p. 109.

33. From Yeats' poem "Before the World Was Made" in *The Collected Poems of W. B. Yeats* (London: Macmillan, 1961), p. 308. See my discussion of his ideas of "mask" and "mirror" in *A Search for God in Time and Memory*, pp. 62, 139–40, 143, and 149–50.

34. I have four translations before me: E. Allison Peers, *The Complete Works of St. John of the Cross*, vols. 1–3 (London: Burns Oates & Washbourne, 1957); Roy Campbell, *Poems of St. John of the Cross* (New York: Grosset & Dunlap, 1967); John Frederick Nims, *The Poems of St. John of the Cross* (Chicago and London: University of Chicago Press, 1979); and Willis Barnstone, *The Poems of Saint John of the Cross* (New York: New Directions, 1972). I am using the Spanish text in San Juan de la Cruz, *Poesías Completas*, ed. by Cristobal Cuevas (Barcelona: Ediciones B, 1988).

35. Here I am translating the poem that begins "Oh llama de amor viva" in San Juan de la Cruz, *Poesías Completas*, pp. 101–102.

36. "Canciones de el alma en la íntima communicación de unión de amor de Dios," ibid., p. 101.

37. Here I am translating the poem that begins "En una noche obscura," ibid., pp. 99–101.

38. "Canciones de el alma que se goza de haber llegado al alto estado de la perfección, que es la unión con Dios, par el camino de la negación espiritual," ibid., p. 99.

39. See my discussion of Heidegger on *Gelassenheit* in my *Peace of the Present*, p. 18.

40. "Noche del sentido" and "Noche del espiritu" in *Poesías Completas,* p. 213.

41. F. Scott Fitzgerald, *The Crack-Up,* p. 75.

42. Saint Augustine, *Confessions,* Book 11, chap. 29 (Chadwick, p. 244).

43. John Adams, *Harmonium* (New York: Associated Music Publishers, 1984). It is a setting of texts by John Donne ("Negative Love") and Emily Dickinson ("Because I Could Not Stop for Death" and "Wild Nights").

44. Adams, *Harmonium,* p. ii.

Love's Mind

1. See my discussion of the "cunning of reason" in *The Peace of the Present,* p. 33.

2. See George Steiner, *Martin Heidegger* (New York: Viking, 1979), p. 15.

3. See Lewis Shiner's novel about the abandoned cities of the Yucatan, *Deserted Cities of the Heart* (New York: Bantam, 1991).

4. Steiner, *Martin Heidegger,* p. 158. See my discussion in *The Peace of the Present,* p. 18.

5. See my discussion of "Thinking is thanking" in *The Peace of the Present,* pp. 18–19.

6. Dante, *Paradiso,* Canto 33, line 145 in E. Moore and Paget Toynbee, *Le Opere di Dante Alighieri* (Oxford: Oxford University Press, 1963), p. 153 (my translation).

7. Pascal, *Pensées,* fragment #68 (#205 in the Brunschvicg edition) in Pascal, *Oeuvres Completes,* ed. by Louis Lafuma (Paris: Editions du Seuil, 1963), p. 508 (my translation).

8. Tolkien, *The Lord of the Rings,* p. 1122.

9. Antonio Salieri, *Prima la musica, pòi le parole* (vocal score in Italian and German), ed. by Josef Heinzelmann and Friedrich Wanek (London and New York: Schott, 1972).

10. Shakespeare, *The Taming of the Shrew,* act 1, line 36 (p. 87 in *The Pelican Shakespeare*).

11. Carlos Fuentes in his introduction to Artur Lundkvist, *Journeys in Dream and Imagination,* p. 15.

12. Saint Augustine, *Confessions,* Book 11, chaps. 14 and 27 (in Chadwick, pp. 230 and 241).

13. Saint Augustine, *The City of God,* Book 15, chap. 22. I am using the Loeb edition by Philip Levine, vol. 5 (Cambridge, Mass.: Harvard, 1966), p. 544, but the translation is mine. See Chadwick's note in Saint Augustine, *Confessions,* on p. 45, "The only surviving verse from his pen is three lines of an evening hymn sung at the lighting of the candle (*City of God* 15.22)."

14. See my discussion of rest in restlessness in *Time and Myth,* p. 79.

15. Martin Buber, *Ecstatic Confessions,* ed. by Paul Mendes-Flohr, trans. by Esther Cameron (San Francisco: Harper & Row, 1985), p. 11.

16. Tolkien, *The Lord of the Rings,* p. 439.

17. T. S. Eliot, *Four Quartets,* p. 27 ("East Coker," line 98).

18. Thomas Hood, "I remember" in *The Serious Poems of Thomas Hood* (London: George Newnes, 1901), p. 7.

19. Dante, *Inferno*, Canto 1 (in Moore and Toynbee, pp. 1–2).

20. Leon Bloy, *Pilgrim of the Absolute*, selections by Raïssa Maritain, trans. by John Coleman and Harry Lorin Binsse (New York: Patheon, 1947), p. 349. See my discussion in *Peace of the Present*, p. 103.

21. Tolkien, *The Lord of the Rings*, p. 815.

22. The motto of the BBC, written in 1927 by Montague John Rendall, one of the first Governors of the Corporation.

23. Tolkien, *The Lord of the Rings*, pp. 397, 747, and 1011 (I am linking the gift of Galadriel in the first two passages with the gift of Arwen in the last).

24. Marthinus Versfeld, *A Guide to the City of God* (London and New York: Sheed & Ward, 1958), p. 2.

25. Aristotle, *Nicomachean Ethics*, trans. by H. Rackham (London: Heinemann, and New York: Putnam, 1926), pp. 12 and 14 (1095b18–29) (the three lives) and pp. 612–628 (1177a–1179b) (the contemplative life as the happy life).

26. W. H. Auden, "In Memory of W. B. Yeats" in W. H. Auden, *Collected Poems*, ed. by Edward Mendelson (New York: Vintage, 1991), p. 249.

27. Leo Bersani and Ulysse Dutoit, *The Forms of Violence* (New York: Schocken, 1985), p. 123 (this chapter, pp. 110–125, is entitled "The Restlessness of Desire"). See my discussion in *The Homing Spirit*, pp. 32–42.

28. Thomas Kelly speaks of "one who practices the perpetual return of the soul into the inner sanctuary, who brings the world into its Light and rejudges it, who brings the Light into the world with all its turmoil and its fitfulness and recreates it" in *A Testament of Devotion* (New York: Harper & Row, 1941), p. 35.

29. Helen Waddell, *Poetry in the Dark Ages*, p. 26.

30. T. E. Lawrence, *Seven Pillars of Wisdom* (Harmondsworth, England: Penguin and Jonathan Cape, 1971), p. 364. See my discussion in *Reasons of the Heart*, p. 1.

Index

Adams, John, 104
Adler, Alfred, 74
Adorno, Theodore, 69, 77
Aeneid (Virgil), 74, 75
Alcuin, 80, 95
Alfred the Great (king of Wessex),
   81
Ambrose (saint), 112
Ancient Voices of Children (Garcia
   Lorca and Crumb), 82
Anderson, Barbara, 6
Aquinas, Thomas. *See* Thomas
   Aquinas (saint)
Aristotle, 118
Arnold, Matthew, 28
"Attention is the natural prayer
   of the soul," 42–43, 86–87,
   102–3, 104, 120
Augustine (saint)
   city of God of, 112–13, 117, 118
   and direction of love, 12, 103
   duality of knowing and
      unkowing love, 104
   end of story of his life, 35
   on listening to music, 44
   and love of God, 84
   method of prayer, 61, 62
   reading of, 94, 136 n
   remembering God, 59, 60, 85,
      87
   remembering his life, 19
   restless heart of, 58, 112–13, 119
   and voice of a person before
      God, 34

Ayasofya (Hagia Sophia), 48–49,
   123, 125–34

Bach, Johann Sebastian, 49, 50
Bacon, Francis, 59, 62
Barthes, Roland, 71, 95
Becket, Thomas, 79
Beethoven, Ludwig von, 9, 36, 43,
   44, 46, 50, 111
Being and Time (Heidegger), 64
Benjamin, Walter, 10–14, 16, 19,
   21–22, 27, 86
Berg, Alban, 77
Bersani, Leo, 119
Bible
   Gospel of John, 15, 18, 22, 41,
      42, 59, 79, 82, 93
   Gospel of Luke, 40
   Song of Solomon, 76, 97
   Song of Songs, 76
   Wisdom of Sirach, 27
   Wisdom of Solomon, 27
Bloy, Leon, 20, 117
Blue Road, The (White), 17
Böll, Heinrich, 55
Boredom, 16–17
Borges, Jorge Luis, 76
Broch, Hermann, 72–73, 75, 76,
   79, 81–82
Brod, Max, 38, 39
Buber, Martin, 41, 68, 113
Byatt, A. S., 83

Camus, Albert, 23
Celan, Paul, 46, 86, 87

City of God (Augustine), 103, 112, 117, 118
Claudel, Paul, 45
Cloud of Unknowing, The, 88, 89
Confessions (Augustine), 12, 19, 34, 44, 58, 61, 62, 84, 85, 87, 103
Conrad, Joseph, 20, 102
Contemplation
  eye of contemplation, 3
  life of action, 118, 120
  life of contemplation, 118, 119, 120
  life of enjoyment, 118, 120
  and memory, 53, 59
  realms of contemplation, 118–19
  three movements of contemplation, 53–82
  and violence, 118–19
Conversations (Malebranche), 86
Crumb, George, 82

Dante Alighieri, 20, 28, 49, 75–78, 108, 110, 116, 120
"Dark Night" (John of the Cross), 95, 100–101
Dark Night of the Soul (John of the Cross), 24
David (king of Judah and Israel), 50
Death
  as "a mirror of scorn and pity," 55, 80–81
  death's road, 94, 115, 116
  as end of story and song, 67
  and love, 21, 26, 28, 88, 94–95
  and passion of a life, 75–76
  and silence, 58
Death and Transfiguration (Strauss), 69
Death of Virgil, The (Broch), 72–73, 75, 76, 81–82
Deconstruction, 32, 41–42
Derrida, Jacques, 42
Desire. *See* Heart, heart's desire
Divine Comedy, The (Dante), 75, 108
Doctor Faustus (Mann), 71
Donne, John, 58, 104
Don Quixote, 57

Dream of Gerontius, The (Elgar), 75
Dream of Gerontius, The (Newman), 75
Dunbar, William, 92
Dymant, Dora, 39

Eckhart, Meister, 15, 84
Elgar, Edward, 74, 75
Eliot, T. S., 32–34, 36, 46, 51, 69, 111, 115
Erikson, Erik, 35–36

Faith
  and basic trust, 36
  and love, 6–7, 26, 88
  as the marriage of God and the soul, 27
  reading with faith, 40
Fitzgerald, F. Scott, 85, 102
Forms of Violence, The (Bersani), 119
Forster, E. M., 43, 44, 75, 111
Four Horsemen of the Apocalypse, 103
Four Last Songs (Strauss), 69
Four Quartets (Eliot), 46
Friendship, way of spiritual, 65, 67–68, 81
Frost, Robert, 123
Fuentes, Carlos, 112

Garcia Lorca, Federico, 82, 83
George IV (king of England), 66
Geronimo, 35
God
  companionship of, 9, 28
  friends of, 9–29, 110
  as a guarding presence, 20–29, 109–10
  as a guiding presence, 10–20, 109–10
  journey with, 9, 10, 15, 19, 22, 28, 81
  love of, 4, 5, 6–7, 11–12, 29, 75, 86, 90, 94, 97, 103
  lovers of, 10, 83–105
  in memory, 28, 85–86, 87, 119
  negative way to, 55, 62, 104–5, 107, 108, 113, 119, 120

proof of the existence of, 28
reunion with, 13–15, 17
"surrounded by silence" of, 14
unconditional love of, 2
voice of the person before God, 34
wrestling with, 10, 19
Gorky, Max, 60
Gregorian chants, 43

Hallaj, al- (Abu al-Mughith al-Husayn ibn Mansur al-Hallaj), 11
Hammarskjöld, Dag, 14, 21, 25, 27
Harmonium (Adams), 104
Haskins, M. L., 66
Heart
    being outside one's heart, 18
    city of the heart, 108–9, 117, 120
    divided heart, 9, 10
    following the heart, 72–82, 96, 115
    heart's desire (heart's longing), 16–17, 19, 23, 26, 29, 32, 34, 35, 48, 50, 52, 55, 60, 61, 73, 80–81, 89, 97, 99–101, 103, 107, 108, 110–16, 119
    heart speaks to heart, 103, 114, 117, 963–72
    music from the heart, 9
    ordeal of the human heart, 9 10
    places in the heart, 20, 109, 117–18, 119
    purity of, 22–23, 27, 112, 113
    restlessness of the heart, 54–63, 119
    thoughts of the heart, 37, 38, 39–41, 47
Heart of Darkness (Conrad), 21, 102
Hegel, Georg Wilhelm Friedrich, 107
Heidegger, Martin
    and death, 67, 70, 96
    and *Gelassenheit* (letting be), 101–2

mystery shown and withdrawn, 5, 52
and paths leading to nowhere, 108, 109
and time, 60, 64, 70
Hölderlin, Friedrich, 139 n
Hood, Thomas, 116
Howards End (Forster), 43
Hymns to the Night (Novalis), 123

Imagination, 25, 47, 71–72, 78
Isaiah, 40
Islandia (Wright), 68

Jacob, Max, 77
Jazz, 45, 46
John of Salisbury, 79
John of the Cross (saint), 24, 27, 87–88, 95–96, 97–102
Jonson, Ben, 3, 38
Judson, Sylvia, 3
Juliana of Norwich, 36
Jung, Carl Gustav, 91

Kafka, Franz, 38, 39, 49, 50, 86
Kandinsky, Wassily, 94
Kant, Immanuel, 89
Ker, W. P., 78
Kierkegaard, Søren, 6, 23, 27, 28, 52, 67, 93
Knowledge
    desire to know, 37, 38
    knowing and unknowing love, 1–6, 74–75, 83, 88–89, 104, 107, 120
    "we can know more than we can tell," 58, 60
Kristeva, Julia, 6

Lacan, Jacques, 49
Lawrence, T. E., 4, 103, 120
Leonardo da Vinci, 61, 62
Lewis, C. S., 66
Lilith (MacDonald), 22, 25–26
"Little Gidding" (Eliot), 36

Love
   "All love is lost but upon God
      alone," 92
   conflicts of, 10
   and death, 21, 26, 28, 88, 94–95
   detachment in, 6
   direction of, 12, 15, 20–21,
      27–28, 29, 80, 90, 92, 102–3,
      105, 114, 120
   freedom toward, 77–78
   and grief, 20–21
   intimate and lasting, 55, 58,
      60–61, 90, 118
   knowing and unknowing love,
      1–6, 74–75, 83, 88–89, 104,
      107, 120
   and lost loves, 15
   love's mind, 2, 5, 74, 107–21
   love's road, 21, 58, 80–81, 82,
      93, 94–105, 108–9, 117
   negative love, 55, 62, 104–5,
      107, 108, 113, 119, 120
   Platonic love, 50
   remembering love, 84–94, 98,
      115–16, 119
   "to be heart-free in love,"
      116–17
   uncertainty in, 5
Lover's Discourse, A (Barthes), 95
Lukacs, Georg, 27
Luke, Helen, 77
Lundkvist, Artur, 53, 54, 57, 76

MacDonald, George, 22, 23–24,
   25–26, 60, 97
McKillip, Patricia, 6
Malebranche, Nicolas, 86, 87
Mann, Thomas, 71
Marceau, Marcel, 56, 57, 58, 59
Marcus Aurelius (Roman
   emperor), 91–92
Markings (Hammarskjöld), 21
Mathes, Carl, 134 n
Meditations (Marcus Aurelius),
   91–92
"Memorial of Access" (Bacon), 62
"Merle and the Nightingale, The"
   (Dunbar), 92

Midsummer Night's Dream, A
   (Shakespeare), 1–2, 3, 5
Modersohn, Otto, 69
Mozart, Wolfgang Amadeus, 26,
   28, 29, 42–44, 46, 47, 50, 51,
   111, 120
Music, way of
   composing music, 43, 44, 46, 67
   "First the music, then the
      words," 31, 111
   and improvization, 46–47, 111
   listening to music, 43–44
   and meaning of words, 42–43
   music and the passion of a life,
      43, 44, 45, 48, 49, 111
   music as a state of being, 45–46,
      47, 50
   music as symbolic form, 45–46,
      47, 50
   and spiritual friendship, 65
   spontaneous song, 47
   as a way to the essence of
      knowing, 31, 32, 51

"Negative Love" (Donne), 104
Newman, John Henry, 9, 10, 18,
   27, 75, 90
Night
   "the night of sense," 21, 22, 24,
      102, 104
   "the night of the spirit," 21, 22,
      24–25, 102, 104
Not First in Nobody's Heart (Paquin
   and Doherty), 96
Nouwen, Henri, 55
Novalis (Friedrich von
   Hardenberg), 22, 77,
   123

O'Keeffe, Georgia, 68
"O Live Flame of Love" (John of
   the Cross), 95, 98–99
On Being and Essence (Thomas
   Aquinas), 4
"On Fairy-Stories" (Tolkein), 35
On Music (Augustine), 44, 136 n
On Reading (Proust), 31, 34

Paradiso (Dante), 20

Particulars of My Life (Skinner), 63

Pascal, Blaise, 110

Phantastes (MacDonald), 22, 23

Pierrot Lunaire (Schönberg), 70

Pilate, Pontius, 79

Pindar, 71

Plato, 14, 43, 44

Poetry in the Dark Ages (Waddell), 81

Polanyi, Michael, 58, 60, 61–62

Possession (Byatt), 83

Prayer
"attention is the natural prayer of the soul," 42–43, 86–87, 102–3, 104, 120
as conscious desire, 61
spontaneous prayer, 47
true language of prayer, 50, 51
voice of prayer, 40

Prelude in C (Bach), 49

Prima la musica, poi le parole (Salieri), 111

Proust, Marcel, 18, 31, 32, 33, 34, 35, 36, 37, 39, 40, 41, 49, 59, 85, 86, 88, 89, 93, 94, 95, 112

Purity of Heart Is to Will One Thing (Kierkegaard), 23

Quakers, "inner light" of, 87, 110, 120

Quiet eye, 3–4, 5, 6

Reading. *See* Words, way of

Religion
religion as anxiety, 51–52
religion as tranquillity, 51

Remembrance of Things Past (Proust), 18, 85

Restlessness of the heart, 54–63, 119

Richard II (Shakespeare), 33

Rilke, Rainer Maria, 53

Road Goes Ever On, The (Tolkein), 68

"Road Not Taken, The" (Frost), 123

"Road Past the View" (O'Keeffe), 68

Roads
death's road, 94, 115, 116
high road and low road, 115, 116
love's road, 21, 58, 80–81, 82, 93, 94–105, 108–9, 117
roads taken and not taken, 16, 31, 58, 109, 111, 123–24
"the road goes ever on and on," 16, 68, 69
"the road of spiritual negation," 101
"the road of the union of love with God," 7, 16, 17, 21, 27, 65, 68, 81, 91, 96, 99, 101, 117
"the road which makes death a fulfillment," 21

Salieri, Antonio, 31, 111

Samuel, 87

Schönberg, Arnold, 70

Schubert, Franz, 65–68, 77, 78, 111

Science and Human Behavior (Skinner), 63

Shakespeare, William, 1–2, 3, 5, 33, 34, 38, 47, 60, 63, 108, 111

Skinner, B. F., 63

Soliloquies (Augustine), 61, 62

Solovyov, Vladimir, 48

Song cycles
Adams, *Harmonium*, 104
composition of, 31, 111, 123–24
Dunne, *Ayasofya (Songs to Holy Wisdom)*, 123, 125–34
Dunne, *Songs about Songs*, 123–24, 134–40
Elgar, *The Dream of Gerontius*, 75
Garcia Lorca and Crumb, *Ancient Voices of Children*, 82
Schönberg, *Pierrot Lunaire*, 70
Schubert, *The Winter Journey*, 68–69
Strauss, *Four Last Songs*, 69
Stravinsky, *Symphony of Psalms*, 49, 52

Song cycles (*continued*)
Tolkein, *The Road Goes Ever On*, 68
"Songs of the Soul in the Intimate Communication of Union of Love of God" (John of the Cross), 98–99
"Songs of the Soul that Rejoices at Having Attained to the High State of Perfection, That Is Union with God, by the Road of Spiritual Negation" (John of the Cross), 101
"Spiritual Canticle" (John of the Cross), 95
Steiner, George, 109
Stewart, Mary, 69
Stories of God (Rilke), 53
Storytelling
cycles of, 12–13
as a mirror, 55
Strauss, Richard, 69
Stravinsky, Igor, 49, 52
Sullivan, Kristen, 124 n
Summas (Thomas Aquinas), 4, 55
Symphony of Psalms (Stravinsky), 49, 52

Teresa of Avila (saint), 29
"Thinking is thanking" (*Denken ist Danken*), 109
Thomas, Dylan, 89
Thomas Aquinas (saint), 1, 2, 4, 6, 32, 33, 53, 55, 76, 86, 94
"Three Meetings" (Solovyov), 48
Time
constitutive time, 27–28
and eternity, 14–15, 27–28, 43, 45, 51–52, 65, 67, 112
lost and found time, 34
time as a horizon, 64–65, 70
timeless presence in, 18
time of storytelling, 16
"time out of mind," 91
time's arrow, 12, 18, 27–28
time turning into space, 17
Tolkein, J. R. R., 10, 11, 16, 17, 19, 20, 35, 53, 55, 63, 68, 70,

84–85, 90, 109, 110, 114, 117, 118
Tolstoy, Leo, 60, 81
Trakl, Georg, 94, 96
Transfigured Night (Schönberg), 70
Troilus and Cressida (Shakespeare), 33
Turner, W. J., 26, 29, 42, 44

Unconscious, 74
Upanishads, 55

Valery, Paul, 61
Versfeld, Martin, 18, 118
Violence and contemplation, 118–19
Virgil, 79–80
Vision, A (Yeats), 47–48, 97

Waddell, Helen, 78, 79–80, 81, 107
Weil, Simone, 12, 52, 102
White, Kenneth, 17
Winchester House, 33
Winter Journey, The (Schubert), 68–69
Words, way of
as "a communication in the midst of solitude," 37–40, 59, 95–96
intimate communication, 99
lectio divina (divine reading), 39, 40, 112
and reading, 31, 32, 35, 36, 37–38, 41, 59, 94, 95, 112
silence and mime, 56, 57–58, 59
and spiritual friendship, 65
tacit dimension of, 58
"the word beyond speech," 82, 84
three voices of poetry, 32–38, 111
as a way to the essence of knowing, 31, 32, 34
Wordsworth, William, 92
Wright, A. T., 68

Yeats, William Butler, 47–48, 73, 97